ALMOST
impossible
puzzles

ALMOST
impossible
puzzles

More than **150** fiendish puzzles
to pit your wits against

TIM SOLE

SIRIUS

SIRIUS

This edition published in 2024 by Sirius Publishing, a division of
Arcturus Publishing Limited,
26/27 Bickels Yard, 151–153 Bermondsey Street,
London SE1 3HA

ISBN: 978-1-3988-4500-8
AD011840NT

Printed in China

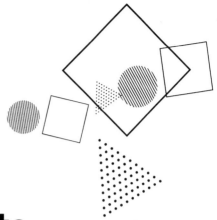

contents

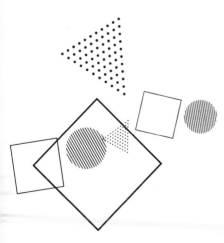

AckNowLedgMeNts

My thanks are due to many people, without whose help this book would not have happened. One in particular stands out: Rod Marshall created, assisted with, or brought to my attention a significant proportion of the puzzles within. He is a very talented person.

   Apologies in advance if I have overlooked anyone, but for creating, assisting with, or suggesting the following puzzles I thank: 12-Roger Gilbert, 20-Chris Munro, 22-Tad Dunne, 35-Roger Gilbert, 37-Roger Gilbert, 39-H. E. Dudeney, 46-Terry Wills, 57-Maurice Steinhart, 61-Charles G. Groeschell, 71-Roger Gilbert, 76-Henry Garfath, 89-Heather Marshall, 90-Maurice Steinhart, 97-Terry Wills, 98-Roger Gilbert and P. C. Wickens, 99-Alan Wilson, 109-Danny Roth, 123-Paul McHugh, 126-Chris Cole, 130-Dennis Lister, 134-Maurice Steinhart, 136-Phil Watson and Kevin Kelly, 137-Roger Gilbert, 153-Alan Wilson, John Gemmell, Tom Grimes, 155-L.J. Gray and 161-David Wharton.

   Lastly, because she really is

      2 wonderful

      2 me

      2 ever be

      <u>4</u> got

    10, I thank my wife Judy.

Tim Sole
timsole@icloud.com

puzzle 1

Find a ten-digit number whose first digit is the number of ones in the number, whose second digit is the number of twos in the number, whose third digit is the number of threes in the number, and so on up to the tenth digit, which is the number of zeros in the number.

puzzle 2

Would it be easier for a helicopter to take off from the surface of the moon or the surface of the Earth?

puzzle 3

From a set of 45 double-8 dominoes (see table opposite), four dominoes are missing. The pattern below is made from the remaining 41 dominoes. The eight numbers on the four missing dominoes are: 1, 1, 2, 4, 4, 5, 5 and 6.

			3	7	5	3	
		1	0	2	7	2	0
		7	0	░	░	1	8
		7	4	░	░	5	8
		2	1	░	░	6	6
		7	6	0	8	8	4
		0	4	2	8	0	4
				6	5		
3	8	5	4	8	6	3	7
2	4	4	7	6	3	2	7
8	7	1	░	░	1	8	8
0	0	1	░	░	3	1	3
5	6	1	░	░	0	0	3
	2	2	5	7	3	6	
	5	5	4	3	2	6	

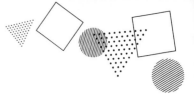

Identify the position of each domino and name the missing dominoes.

To help you, a full set of double-8 dominoes looks like this	0-0	0-1	0-2	0-3	0-4	0-5	0-6	0-7	0-8
	1-1	1-2	1-3	1-4	1-5	1-6	1-7	1-8	2-2
	2-3	2-4	2-5	2-6	2-7	2-8	3-3	3-4	3-5
	3-6	3-7	3-8	4-4	4-5	4-6	4-7	4-8	5-5
	5-6	5-7	5-8	6-6	6-7	6-8	7-7	7-8	8-8

puzzle 4

The magic square below has a hole in the middle and uses 24 dominoes from a set of 28 dominoes. Before 12 numbers were blanked out, the numbers in each row and each column added up to 21.

	6	1	5	3	0	
1		2	5	3		6
2	6	2		3	1	6
4	3		▓		2	3
5	6	0		4	4	0
2		6	2	4		2
	0	5	6	0	5	

The blanked-out numbers are: 0, 0, 1, 1, 2, 3, 3, 4, 4, 4, 5 and 5, and the eight numbers on the four missing dominoes are: 0, 1, 1, 1, 3, 4, 5 and 6. Identify the position of each domino in the magic square and name the missing dominoes.

To help you, a full set of dominoes looks like this						
0-0	0-1	0-2	0-3	0-4	0-5	0-6
1-1	1-2	1-3	1-4	1-5	1-6	2-2
2-3	2-4	2-5	2-6	3-3	3-4	3-5
3-6	4-4	4-5	4-6	5-5	5-6	6-6

puzzle 5

A hundred treasure chests have been arranged in a circle and are numbered from 1 to 100 in ascending order. Initially the lids of the treasure chests are all shut.

On the first walk around the circle, beginning with treasure chests one and two, the lid of each chest is opened.

On the second walk around the circle the lid of every second treasure chest is closed (2, 4, 6, 8 etc).

On the third walk around the circle the lid of every third treasure chest is opened if it was closed and closed if it was open (3, 6, 9, 12 etc).

On the fourth walk around the circle the lid of every fourth treasure chest is closed if it was open and opened if it was closed (4, 8, 12, 16 etc).

And so on, until there have been 100 walks around the circle.

At this point the treasure chests with their lids closed are taken away and you are invited to help yourself to as much treasure as you want so long as you don't take treasure from 10% or more of the remaining treasure chests. How many treasure chests could you take treasure from?

puzzle 6

P and Q are five-digit numbers that between them contain all ten digits, as does their product, P X Q. If P = 54,321, what is Q?

puzzle 7

A series of fun runs are being held on a circular route with a circumference of 31 miles. There are six refreshment stations on the route, which between them also serve as start and finishing points for the various races. The stations are positioned so that whatever race is being run, from 1 mile, 2 miles, 3 miles, and so on up to 30 miles, there will be two stations that are that distance apart from one another.

Relative to each other, where might the refreshment stations be positioned around the circular route?

puzzle 6

When the examination results were published, one college found that all 32 of its students were successful in at least one of the three exams that each of them had taken. Of the students who did not pass Exam One, the number who passed Exam Two was exactly half of the number who passed Exam Three. The number who passed only Exam One was the same as the number who passed only one of the other two exams, and three more than the number who passed Exam One and at least one of the other two exams.

How many students passed more than one exam?

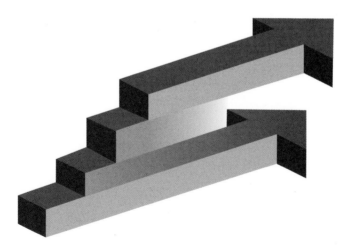

puzzle 9

A game board has 28 holes arranged as shown below. The game starts with a peg in every hole except the central one (shaded in the diagram) and is played like solitaire. Each move consists of jumping in a straight line over an adjacent peg into a hole that is adjacent to the peg being jumped over. The peg that has just been jumped over is then removed from the board. The game ends when there are no more jumps available to the player or players.

It is impossible to finish this game with just one peg on the board. True or false?

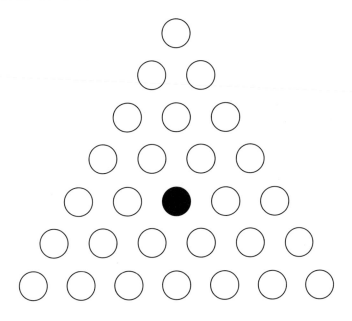

puzzle 10

A number of identical planes, each of which has a tank that will hold just enough fuel to travel halfway around the world, are based on a small island. If the planes can only refuel from the island or from another plane of their fleet, what is the smallest number of planes that would be required for one plane to complete a great circle around the world, with each plane involved in the operation returning safely to the island?

Assume that planes can refuel and transfer fuel instantaneously, and that all planes travel at the same constant speed.

puzzle 11

100 passengers are boarding a 100-passenger plane. Of those 100 passengers, 98 have ordered normal meals, and the other two, Hassan and Susie, have ordered special meals.

The first passenger to board the plane is Hassan. Hassan left his glasses in his bag and cannot read the seat number on his boarding pass. He sits in a seat at random.

The next 98 passengers to board the plane have all ordered normal meals and they take their seats on the plane one after another. Each sits in the seat assigned to them or, if it is occupied, they sit in an unoccupied seat at random.

The last passenger to board the plane is Susie, and she sits in the last available seat.

All passengers accept the meal that is delivered to them. Assuming no mistakes by the air stewards, what is the probability of (a) Hassan receiving a special meal and (b) Susie receiving a special meal?

puzzle 12

Joe and Donald played a 25-game tournament of horseshoes. To decide the winner of the tournament, instead of counting the number of games each player won, they counted the overall number of points scored.

Joe started the first game, and after that, the player to throw first was the person who won the previous game. (None of the games were tied.) Over the course of the 25 games, Joe won six of the games in which he threw first, and Donald won seven of the games in which he threw first.

After 24 games, Joe and Donald had each scored the same number of points. Which player won the 25th game, and therefore the tournament?

puzzle 13

A long time ago, £1 would buy eight hens or one sheep, and £10 would buy one cow. A farmer buying animals of each type bought a hundred animals for £100. Which animals did the farmer buy?

puzzle 14

Seven friends stranded on a desert island start arguing about what day of the week it is.

- ➤ Axel thinks that yesterday was Wednesday.

- ➤ Fergal disagrees, saying that tomorrow is Wednesday.

- ➤ Hans maintains that the day after tomorrow is Tuesday.

- ➤ Pierre feels sure that yesterday was not Friday.

- ➤ Mohammad believes that today is Tuesday.

- ➤ Leo says that today is not Sunday, Monday or Tuesday.

- ➤ Carlos is adamant that it is Tuesday tomorrow.

If just one of them is right, what day of the week is it?

puzzle 15

If the pattern continued, what would be the ninth line in the pyramid below?

```
                    1
                 1     1
                 2     1
              1  2  1  1
           1  1  1  2  2  1
           3  1  2  2  1  1
        1  3  1  1  2  2  2  1
     1  1  1  3  2  1  3  2  1  1
```

--- ○ ◑ ◐ ◑ ○ ○ ---

puzzle 16

Using exactly four fours and no other numbers, find an expression that is equal to zero. You may use brackets as required and as many of the symbols for addition, subtraction, multiplication and division as you need, but no others.

That was easy. Now do the same for the integers from one to ten.

puzzle 17

As with the previous puzzle, but this time for the integers from 11 to 30 and with the symbols for decimal point and square root also being available if required.

○ ○ ◍ ◑ ◍ ○ ○

puzzle 18

A five-digit security code is such that in each of the following numbers, one and only one of the digits is in the same position as the security code.

| 06582 | 19086 | 24937 | 32023 | 45900 |
| 58064 | 67123 | 71657 | 81459 | 96880 |

So we can tell from looking at the first number on the list, 06582, that 00000 and 28560 are possible security codes, but 11111 (which has no matches with 06582) and 06999 (which has two matches) are not. What is the security code?

puzzle 19

From a set of 45 double-8 dominoes (see table below), four dominoes are missing. The pattern opposite is made from the remaining 41 dominoes. The eight numbers on the four missing dominoes are: 0, 1, 2, 4, 5, 5, 5 and 7.

Identify the position of each domino and name the missing dominoes.

To help you, a full set of double-8 dominoes looks like this								
0-0	0-1	0-2	0-3	0-4	0-5	0-6	0-7	0-8
1-1	1-2	1-3	1-4	1-5	1-6	1-7	1-8	2-2
2-3	2-4	2-5	2-6	2-7	2-8	3-3	3-4	3-5
3-6	3-7	3-8	4-4	4-5	4-6	4-7	4-8	5-5
5-6	5-7	5-8	6-6	6-7	6-8	7-7	7-8	8-8

	6	4	2	7	
5	1	3	7	4	2
8	0			0	0
1	7			0	8
8	5			4	8
3	5	5	3	6	2
8	4	7	4	5	8
		6	1		

6	2	8	7	2	5	6	8
6	1	1	8	8	4	4	2
7	4	6			3	1	3
0	6	0			3	1	3
0	1	1			0	0	3
	2	3	5	7	3	6	
	2	4	2	6	7	7	

23

puzzle 20

Jill has thought of a number between 13 and 1,300, and Jack is doing his best to guess it. Unbeknownst to Jack, Jill is teasing him by not always answering truthfully.

> ➤ Jack asks whether the number is below 500, and then whether the number is a perfect square. On both occasions, Jill lies.

> ➤ For his third question, Jack asks whether the number is a perfect cube, which Jill answers truthfully, and for his fourth question, Jack asks whether the second digit is a zero.

Jack then states the number that he thinks Jill thought of and, not surprisingly, is wrong. From the information above, name Jill's number.

puzzle 21

Three people were presented with a challenge. From a stock of three red and two yellow balls, three balls were chosen at random, and each was then concealed in a different box. The challenge was for each person in turn to look inside two of the boxes to see if they could determine the hue of the ball in the other box.

   The first person looked inside boxes 1 and 3, but was not able to determine the hue of the ball in box 2. The second person, having watched and heard the first, then looked inside boxes 2 and 3, but could not then determine the hue of the ball in box 1. Having watched and heard persons one and two, the third person then stated the hue of the ball in one of the boxes, without even bothering to look inside the other two.

   Which box did she name, and what was the hue of the ball in it?

puzzle 22

Near the end of a meeting, everyone shakes hands with everybody else. Someone new then arrives and shakes hands with only those people they know, which is not everyone at the meeting. By doing this, the total number of handshakes increases by 25%. How many people at the meeting did the new person know?

puzzle 23

Find a ten-digit number that:

- ➤ Can be described as having m digits between the m's, n digits between the n's, and so on, and

- ➤ Whose first digit is a prime number, the two-digit number formed by its second and third digits is a prime number, the three-digit number formed by its fourth, fifth and sixth digits is three times a prime number, and the four-digit number formed by its last four digits is also a prime number.

puzzle 24

The Golden Bay Dining Tour itinerary includes six dinners. Five people following this itinerary are all at different stages of the tour. One person has dined once so far, and the other four have dined two, three, four and five times. The dining itinerary begins and ends with dinner at The Old School Cafe, and the four dinners between are at four other restaurants and always in the same order.

From this information and the information below, determine for each person where they came from, where on this itinerary they last dined, and where they will be dining next.

> ➤ Anouk, who is not from Christchurch, will dine next at the Farewell Spit Cafe.

> ➤ Bosai does not come from Auckland.

> ➤ Carmen, who last dined at Milliways Restaurant, will not be dining at the Collingwood Tavern next.

> ➤ Diego is not from Auckland or Dunedin, and dined last at somewhere other than the Collingwood Tavern.

> ➤ Eduardo comes from Hamilton.

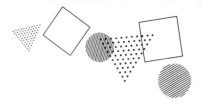

- ➤ The next person to dine at the Wholemeal Cafe did not last dine at the Collingwood Tavern.

- ➤ Bosai, the person from Christchurch, the person who last dined at the Farewell Spit Cafe, and the person who will next dine at Milliways Restaurant are four of the five people.

- ➤ Neither the person from Wellington nor the person from Dunedin will be dining next at the Collingwood Tavern.

puzzle 25

A, B and C each have a hat placed on their head. On each hat is an integer (a whole number) that is greater than zero. Each knows, and that the others know, that they are all experts in logic.

They can see the other two hats but not their own. They are told that the sum of the integers on two of the hats is equal to the number on the third hat.

> A says that she doesn't know the number on her hat.

> B says he doesn't know the number on his hat either.

> C then says that the number on her hat is 25.

What were the integers on A's and B's hats?

puzzle 26

The digital root of a number is obtained by summing its digits and then repeating this process until the answer is a single digit. For example, the digital root of 8777 (and 29) is 2.

Noting that any number divisible by nine has a digital root of nine, what is the digital root of $(9^{6130} + 2)^{4875}$?

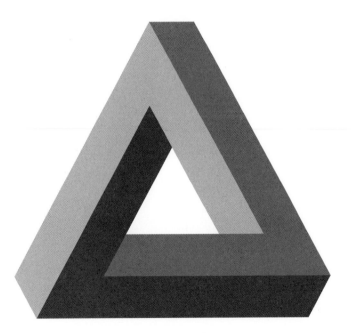

puzzle 27

Any integer from 0 to 102 can be expressed using no more than one each of the following digits, 3, 5, 7 and 9, and the signs for addition, subtraction and multiplication as needed. For example: 3 + 9 − 5 − 7 = 0. Complete the table below:

1	9 − 5 − 3	2		3	3
4		5		6	
7		8		9	
10		11		12	
13		14		15	
16		17		18	
19		20		21	
22		23		24	
25		26		27	
28		29		30	
31		32		33	
34		35		36	
37		38		39	
40		41		42	

43		44		45	
46		47		48	
49		50		51	
52		53		54	
55		56		57	
58		59		60	
61		62		63	
64		65		66	
67		68		69	
70		71		72	
73		74		75	
76		77		78	
79		80		81	
82		83		84	
85		86		87	
88		89		90	
91		92		93	
94		95	95	96	
97		98		99	
100		101		102	

puzzle 26

The papers relating to a life insurance policy included the following note from the salesman:

"There is no explaining the conduct of some of our policyholders. This lady rang me for a policy but then would not tell me the ages of her three children! All she would say was that the product of their ages was three times the number of their house, the sum of their ages was the number of the house next door, and her eldest child had a paper round. When I asked her for her address, she said something about Tow Path Road and then hung up.

Luckily for me, the actuary was visiting our branch that day and he seems to enjoy this sort of problem. I told him what had happened, and explained that Tow Path Road was unusual in that it had houses on one side only, so that house seven, for example, was next door to house numbers six and eight. I then left him to it.

How he reached his decision I will never understand, but shortly after I had explained the problem to him the actuary came to my office and announced that he was just about sure that the children were two, two and nine. As usual, he was right."

Scribbled underneath in what looked like the actuary's handwriting was this message, dated April 1st:

"Nice to see that someone has faith in the actuary. Just to set the record straight, however, the above note needs a correction. Although the children were indeed two, two and nine, the information I used to figure out the children's ages was that the product of the children's ages was three times the number of the house next door and the sum of their ages was the number of their own house."

Was the correction a hoax?

puzzLe 29

A Christmas decoration comprises a symmetrical four-pointed star supported by three threads. The decoration hangs in the middle of a small circular window:

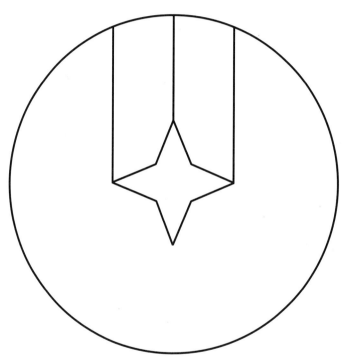

The central thread is 4 cm long, and the outer two are each 6 cm long. What is the width of the star?

puzzle 30

Which of the following poker hands is stronger?

OR

Think about it!

puzzle 31

The pattern below is made from two sets of dominoes. Dominoes from one set are positioned horizontally in the puzzle, and dominoes from the other set are positioned vertically.

Box 1

1	5	3	5	4	1	1
4	5	2	6	3	0	4
4	1	6	6	3	6	6
1	0	5	4	1	3	1

Box 2

2	3	1	2	0	4	2
1	4	6	2	4	3	5
6	6	3	4	4	3	4
2	6	5	6	5	5	2

	5	0	5	1	2	
0	1	3	5	1	2	2
2	0	1	3	3	0	4
	2	3	6	1	0	

Box 3

	0	0	0	0	3	
1	1	4	6	5	3	2
4	2	0	4	4	0	3
	3	0	2	2	0	

Box 4

The numbers blanked out in Box 3 are either all fives or all sixes. Similarly with Box 4. Identify the position of each domino.

38

Horizontal Dominoes						
0-0	0-1	0-2	0-3	0-4	0-5	0-6
1-1	1-2	1-3	1-4	1-5	1-6	2-2
2-3	2-4	2-5	2-6	3-3	3-4	3-5
3-6	4-4	4-5	4-6	5-5	5-6	6-6

Vertical Dominoes						
0 0	0 1	0 2	0 3	0 4	0 5	0 6
1 1	1 2	1 3	1 4	1 5	1 6	2 2
2 3	2 4	2 5	2 6	3 3	3 4	3 5
3 6	4 4	4 5	4 6	5 5	5 6	6 6

puzzle 32

Between noon and midnight, but not counting these times, how often will the minute hand and hour hand of a clock overlap?

○ ○ ◑ ◐ ◑ ○ ○

puzzle 33

One leaf has been torn out of a book. The sum of the remaining page numbers is 10,000. What is the last-numbered page in the book, and which leaf is missing?

puzzle 34

Place the numbers 1 to 19 in the diagram in such a way that the numbers in each of the 15 straight lines of small hexagons have the same total, namely 38. It is not easy, but it can be done!

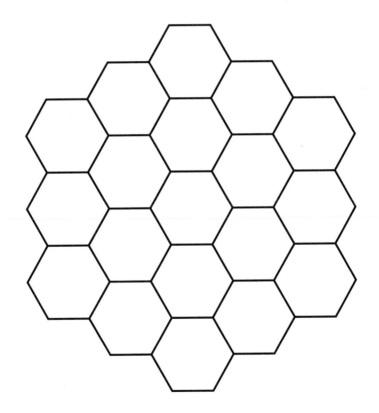

puzzle 35

Pairs from Bluetown competed against pairs from Greytown in a sporting event, but inclement weather meant a low turnout. In a second event the weather was better, and between the two towns 24 extra pairs competed.

Both events featured spot prizes, awarded at random to two individuals who may or may not be from the same pair or from the same town.

As it happened, for each event the probability that the two winners of the spot prizes would be from the same town was exactly 50%. How many competed in the second event?

puzzle 36

Why are 1988 pound coins worth more than 1983 pound coins?

○ ○ ◍ ◐ ◍ ○ ○

puzzle 37

A bowling club has fewer than 100 members. To the nearest whole number, 28% of the members are former committee members, 29% are current committee members, and 42% have never been on the committee. Again to the nearest whole number, 35% of the former committee members are men.
   What is the total membership of the club?

puzzle 30

Security at Prime Palace is a very straightforward affair. There are no keys, just simple bracelets on which are hung five numbers. Access to sensitive areas is then granted by presenting the bracelet in a way that shows a five-digit prime number. Given that a bracelet can be read clockwise or counterclockwise and there are five numbers to start from, the chances of picking a prime number at random can therefore be as low as one in ten.

Sounds simple? Well, as an extra check, you are asked to swap your bracelet for one of the same shade at every door, so you need to know for your shade the full set of possible prime numbers.

Although the system worked well for many years, it was almost abandoned when the queen remarried. The new king simply could not remember his numbers! He therefore was given a special bracelet that always produced a prime however it was presented, and he was never asked to swap bracelets.

What numbers were on the king's bracelet?

puzzle 39

Tom, Dick and Harry met for a picnic. Tom brought 15 items, Dick brought 9 items, and Harry brought 8 coins of equal value to be shared by the other two as a reimbursement for bringing food for him to share.

Assuming the men consumed equal shares of food (and all the items are of equal value), how should the money be divided?

puzzle 40

Find a five-digit palindromic number (a number that equals itself when read backward) that has a remainder of 9 when divided by 10, a remainder of 8 when divided by 9, a remainder of 7 when divided by 8, and so on, and whose digits are all odd.

puzzle 41

A game between two players is based on choosing an unbroken sequence of three outcomes from tossing a coin. The possible outcomes from a single toss are H (Heads) or T (Tails). The coin is tossed as often as necessary until one of the players' chosen sequences occurs.

For example, player A might choose the sequence THT and player B, who must choose something different, might choose HTT. If successive tosses gave, say, TTHHTHT, then A would win the game after the seventh toss. Had the sixth toss been T rather than H, then B would have won.

A has chosen the sequence TTT and B, who was thinking of choosing HHH, changes his mind to HTT. Has B changed his chances of winning the game?

puzzle 42

Seats for a show are allocated individually. The probability that neither of two seats drawn at random will be an aisle seat is a half, and the probability of them both being aisle seats is a twelfth. How many seats are there?

puzzle 43

Losers' Chess is a fun game that often turns in a surprise result. To play it, ignore checks and checkmates, for the object is either to lose all of one's pieces, king included, or to be stalemated (unable to play a move). Players must capture an opponent's piece if they can, but where there is a choice, can choose which. All other rules are the same as for ordinary chess.

Puzzles in Losers' Chess are rare, and ones with an unusual twist like the one below even rarer. This one, by T. R. Dawson, was first published in 1925 in *Das Wochenschach.* In the first analysis it looks like Black can force White to stalemate him, but White, who is playing up the board, can win by forcing Black to cause the stalemate. How?

White to play and win (Losers' Chess rules)

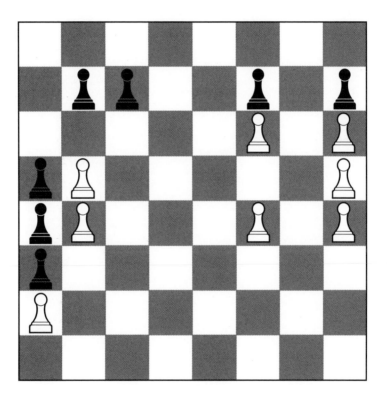

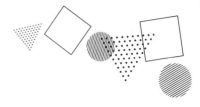

puzzle 44

Using exactly four sevens and no other numbers, find an expression that is equal to 22. You may use brackets as required and as many of the symbols for addition, subtraction, multiplication, division, square root, decimal point, factorial and repeating decimals as required.

puzzle 45

In the boxes below, only one is marked with two true statements, and only one is marked with two false statements.

Box 1	Box 2	Box 3
The treasure is not in here.	The treasure is not in Box 1.	The treasure is not in here.
The treasure is in Box 2.	The treasure is in Box 3.	The treasure is in Box 1.

Which box contains the treasure?

puzzle 46

The Roman numerals still in use are I = 1, V = 5, X = 10, L = 50, C = 100, D = 500, and M = 1000. Examples of Roman numbers are VIII = 8, LXXVI = 76, CXXXVI = 136, and MDCCCLXII = 1862.

Today, the Roman numbers IIII, VIIII, and DCCCC are usually abbreviated as IV, IX, and CM, respectively, a numeral to the left of a higher numeral denoting subtraction. These abbreviations are used in this cross-number, together with CD for CCCC, XC for LXXXX, and XL for XXXX. Thus 1904 would be written as MCMIV and 49 as XLIX.

The logical extension of this method of abbreviation, such as IL for 49, was never fully developed and so is not used here. All that is used, if required, are the abbreviations already mentioned.

In the grid opposite, all answers are Roman numerals and, when converted to Arabic (normal) numbers, are palindromes (none starting with zero) of two digits or more. One palindrome occurs twice; the rest are all different.

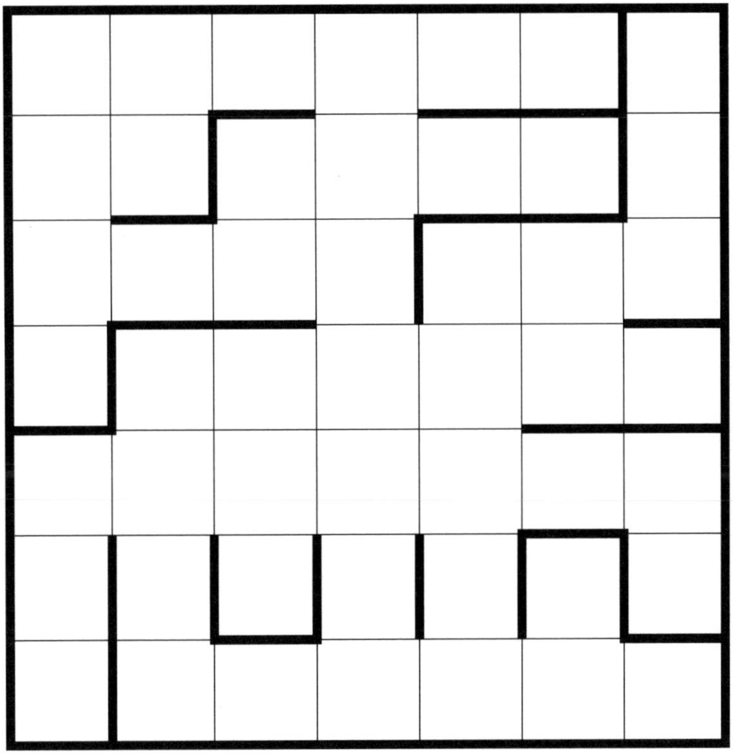

puzzle 47

David's mother has three children. She also has three coins and decides to give one to each child. Penelope is given a penny. Nichola is given a nickel. What is the name of the child who gets the dime?

○ ○ ◍ ◐ ◍ ○ ○

puzzle 48

Allwyn, Aitkin and Arthur are to fight a three-way duel. The order in which they shoot will be determined by lot, and they will continue to shoot until two are dead. Allwyn never misses, Aitkin is 80% accurate, and Arthur, the cleverest of the three, hits his target just half of the time. Who has the best chance of surviving?

puzzle 49

Without using a calculator, determine which is greater:

$$3 \tfrac{1}{8} \times 3 \tfrac{1}{5} \text{ or } 3 \times \sqrt[3]{37}$$

○ ○ ◑ ◐ ◑ ○ ○

puzzle 50

In the expression below, each letter represents a different digit from 1 to 9.

$$\frac{A}{DE} + \frac{B}{FG} + \frac{C}{HI} = 1$$

What are the three fractions?

puzzle 51

Five inventors need to cross a river with their five inventions (one per inventor) using a rowboat that will carry up to three people or inventions in any combination.

The inventors are very secretive about their inventions, and each will not allow their invention to be in the presence of another inventor unless they are present too. All of the inventors can row, as can just one of the inventions, which is a robot. The robot, as well as being able to row, can also load and offload itself and any other inventions from the boat.

Before each crossing begins, the boat must be fully emptied before the boat is loaded up again. How can the five inventors cross the river with their inventions, using just the rowboat?

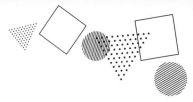

puzzle 52

What are the missing numbers?

31 62 ? 25 56 ? 19

---

puzzle 53

The number 153 is special for at least two reasons. The first has something to do with factorials, and the second has to do with cubes. What are these two reasons?

puzzle 54

A selection of eight cards is dealt, with every second card being returned to the bottom of the pack. Thus the top card goes to the table, card two goes to the bottom of the pack, card three goes to the table, card four to the bottom of the pack, and so on. This procedure continues until all the cards are dealt. The order in which the cards appear on the table is:

AKAKAKAK

How were the cards originally stacked?

puzzle 55

As with Puzzle 54, but starting with 16 cards. When the cards are dealt, the order in which the cards appear on the table is:

AKQJAKQJAKQJAKQJ

How were the cards originally stacked?

puzzle 56

A babysitting club has a system where members use vouchers to pay for babysitting services. One voucher equals one credit, and the cost for babysitting can be anything from 1 to 40 credits (always a whole number).

With up to 40 vouchers required for one babysit, that is a lot of paper. So it has been suggested that vouchers be issued in more than one denomination, and that members use the smaller denominations for giving change when needed.

To reduce the amount of paper needed for any transaction, vouchers would need to be in every denomination from 1 to 40, but that isn't practical. So using as few different voucher denominations as possible, the club is looking for a system that will allow the payment (including the giving of change) for any babysitting service to never need more than one voucher of any given denomination.

What is the minimum number of denominations that can achieve this, and what would those denominations be?

puzzle 57

You have several identical crystals that will shatter if dropped from a certain height or above, but which will remain unscathed if dropped from any height lower than this.

You are in a building that has 106 floors. You have already discovered that a crystal dropped from floor 106 will shatter, but you want to know the lowest floor from which you can drop a crystal so that it will shatter.

You could test one floor at a time, starting from floor one, but to save time you want a quicker way than this, as long as no more than two more crystals will be shattered during the testing. From which floor should you make the first drop, and what is the maximum number of drops you will require?

puzzle 58

Using a rule that can be applied to any natural number, the first ten natural numbers have been arranged into columns as shown below:

1	4	3
2	5	7
6	9	8
10		

Applying this rule, the numbers 11 and 12 would appear in the same column as each other, but which one?

puzzle 59

Flying over a small copse, the pilot looks down and announces that he can see six rows of four trees. "So that is 24 trees?" his passenger asks. "Actually no," says the pilot, "just half that number."
   In what pattern are the trees planted?

puzzle 60

What are the two missing numbers in the series below?

? 3 3 3 7 7 2 3 6 ?

puzzle 61

An insurance company has six account managers, each of whom has a different number of children from none to five. Deduce from the following who has what number of children, which account each manages, and where each lives.

- ➤ Anika has two more children than the manager from Lambeth, who has one more child than the fire manager.

- ➤ The marine manager has two more children than the manager from Enfield, who has one more child than Ebba.

- ➤ The manager from Woolwich has two more children than Dhaval, who has one more child than the automotive manager.

- ➤ Charu has three more children than the property manager.

- ➤ The liability manager has more children than the manager from Croydon, who is not Ebba.

- ➤ The manager from Lambeth, who is not the automotive manager, is not Charu.

- ➤ Ebba is not the property manager, and Felix is not the marine manager.

- ➤ The manager from Brixton may or may not be Bakkar.

- ➤ The manager from Fulham is not the liability manager, but might be the aviation manager.

puzzle 62

The pattern below is made from two sets of dominoes. Dominoes from one set are positioned in the puzzle horizontally, and dominoes from the other set are positioned vertically.

Box 1

1	0	2	0	6	6	1
3	5	0	5	5	5	6
1	3	2	2	3	1	4
1	2	5	5	3	3	1

Box 2

2	2	4	0	1	4	2
4	4	4	3	0	1	1
0	0	6	0	3	5	4
2	6	0	0	3	5	2

	1	6	6	2	2	
3	2	2	5	3	4	0
4	2	1	1	4	4	2
	6	2	1	5	4	

Box 3

	0	3	1	4	4	
3	0	5	3	0	3	1
4	5	1	6	0	6	6
	6	3	4	3	0	

Box 4

The numbers blanked out in Box 3 are either all fives or all sixes. Similarly with Box 4. Identify the position of each domino.

66

Vertical Dominoes

0 0	0 1	0 2	0 3	0 4	0 5	0 6
1 1	1 2	1 3	1 4	1 5	1 6	2 2
2 3	2 4	2 5	2 6	3 3	3 4	3 5
3 6	4 4	4 5	4 6	5 5	5 6	6 6

Horizontal Dominoes

0-0	0-1	0-2	0-3	0-4	0-5	0-6
1-1	1-2	1-3	1-4	1-5	1-6	2-2
2-3	2-4	2-5	2-6	3-3	3-4	3-5
3-6	4-4	4-5	4-6	5-5	5-6	6-6

puzzle 63

A nuclear power station had four missiles to help protect it from attack by air. The missiles were placed 50 miles north, 50 miles east, 50 miles south, and 50 miles west of the power station. Each missile had a range of 70 miles, and was designed to harmlessly self-destruct if it did not hit its target before reaching the end of its range.

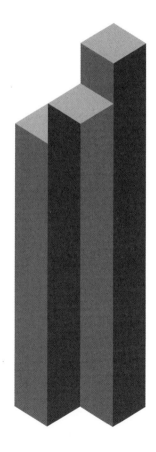

During a training exercise in which each missile was aimed clockwise at the next missile around the power station, the four missiles were accidentally and simultaneously fired, sending them on a spiral route focused on the power station.

If the missiles were to collide above the power station, then the power station would be destroyed. Will the power station survive?

puzzle 64

Reconstruct the following multiplication, using the digits 2, 3, 5 and 7 only.

		X	X	X
			X	X
X	X	X	X	
X	X	X	X	
X	X	X	X	X

puzzle 65

You are given four bags of coins; each bag contains thirteen coins. Two of the bags contain genuine coins only, and the other two bags contain counterfeit coins only.

You know the exact weight of a genuine coin, and you also know that these counterfeit coins, in comparison to genuine coins, will be one or two grams underweight or overweight.

You also know that counterfeit coins in the same bag are identical to one another, but may or may not be identical to the coins in the other counterfeit bag. Taking as many coins from as many bags as you like, how can you identify the two bags of counterfeit coins with a single weighing?

puzzle 66

Continue the sequence:

202 122 232 425 262 728 ? ?

---

puzzle 67

How many squares are there on a chessboard? The answer is not 64!

puzzle 68

A property investor has three daughters, and in his will
he divides his properties among them. The daughters are
excellent logicians.

He calls them together and tells them how many
properties he owns and that each will inherit a different
number of separate properties. He adds that the eldest will
inherit the most properties (but not more than ten) and the
youngest the fewest (with not less than one).

He then whispers in each daughter's ear how many
properties she will inherit. After that, he proceeds from the
eldest daughter to the youngest, asking each daughter if she
can calculate how many properties each of her two sisters
will inherit: each daughter replies "No" in turn. He does this
a second time, and again all three reply "No." But then, when
he asks the question a third time, the eldest daughter says,
"Yes; each of the last two answers gave me some information,
and I now know how many properties my sisters will inherit."

How many properties can each daughter expect to inherit?

puzzle 69

A treasure hunter found the following message:

From Secret Place to Crossbones Rock
Pace out what steps you may.
Turn right at rock and pace the same
And you'll have found Point A.

Return to Secret Place and count
Your steps to Hangman's Tree.
Turn left at tree and now count down
To take you to point B.

Halfway between points A and B
Is buried my treasure case,
But what a shame that you can't know
About my Secret Place.

She knows where Crossbones Rock and Hangman's Tree are located, but not the whereabouts of Secret Place. Can you help her find the buried treasure?

puzzle 70

Five soccer teams, United, County, Rovers, Albion and Thistle, took part in a league tournament. Their uniforms were white, yellow, green, red and blue, but not necessarily in that order. No teams were tied in the standings at the end of the tournament. From the following information, determine each team's captain, uniforms and position in which it finished in the league.

- ➤ Rovers did not win the league, but finished higher than fourth.

- ➤ Neither Albion nor the team in green finished in the top three.

- ➤ Evans captained the team in yellow.

- ➤ Cooke's team finished ahead of County, which was captained by Dixon.

- ➤ Allen's team finished second and Boyle's team finished last.

- ➤ The team in white finished lower than both United and the team in blue, but above Evans's team.

- ➤ Albion was not the green team and United was not the blue team.

puzzle 71

A pond has a flat base and vertical sides. In the middle of the pond, a statue is to be erected using three identical concrete cubes placed side by side as the statue's foundation.

When the first concrete cube is placed flat on the bottom of the pond, the water level rises three inches. When the second and third concrete cubes are placed flat on the bottom of the pond, the water level rises four inches on both occasions. What are the measurements of the cubes?

puzzle 72

Here's one for mathematicians. What is the next term in this series?

10 22 36 55 122 220 ?

puzzle 73

What property having to do with factorials makes the number 145 special?

puzzle 74

The pattern below was made from two sets of 28 dominoes from which seven doubles (0-0, 1-1, 2-2, etc) are missing. The other seven doubles, all different, are either all placed vertically in the pattern or all placed horizontally.

1	1	2	2	1	3
6	3	4	4	3	6
	5	6	6	5	
	1	0	0	5	
5	2	3	3	2	5
1	1	5	5	1	4

0	4	5	4	2	4
3	0	5	1	0	3
	4	6	4	2	
	4	1	6	2	
3	0	6	2	0	1
3	1	6	4	5	3

2	0			2	4
3	5	4	0	3	5
4	5	3	1	0	6
6	2	6	1	0	3
2	0	2	4	6	1
6	0	5	0	6	2

Identify the individual dominoes in the pattern.

Horizontal Dominoes						
0-1	0-2	0-3	0-4	0-5	0-6	1-2
1-3	1-4	1-5	1-6	2-3	2-4	2-5
2-6	3-4	3-5	3-6	4-5	4-6	5-6

Dominoes that are either Horizontal or Vertical						
0-0	1-1	2-2	3-3	4-4	5-5	6-6

Vertical Dominoes						
0 1	0 2	0 3	0 4	0 5	0 6	1 2
1 3	1 4	1 5	1 6	2 3	2 4	2 5
2 6	3 4	3 5	3 6	4 5	4 6	5 6

puzzle 75

If six identical equilateral triangles are joined edge-to-edge, then any of twelve different shapes can be constructed as shown below:

Show that it is impossible to form any six of these shapes into a six-by-six-by-six equilateral triangle.

puzzle 76

A park is in the shape of a semicircle whose diameter is an exact number of yards and less than a mile (1,760 yards). Along its straight side runs a hedge, and on its curved side stand 26 trees.

The distance from the middle of any tree to either end of the hedge is a nonzero, integral number of yards. How long is the hedge?

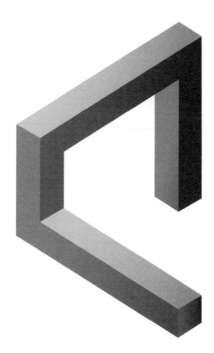

puzzle 77

Three women were stranded on a desert island. This is how they shared the coconuts they found.

The first woman, fearing an argument, decided to take her share secretly in the night. After dividing the coconuts into three equal piles, she had a coconut left over and gave it to the monkey. She then hid her share and put the other two piles back into one big pile. She then went back to sleep.

The second woman, who did not know she had been pre-empted, then did the same thing. That is, she divided the coconuts into three equal piles, found one left over that she gave to the monkey, hid her share, and put the other two piles back into one big pile before going back to sleep.

Lastly for that night, when the third woman woke and the other two were still asleep, she then did the same thing, so there were three secret trips that night and three coconuts for the monkey.

It was obvious to everybody when the sun rose that many of the coconuts were missing, but since each woman was guilty, none of them said anything. Instead, they divided the remaining coconuts into three equal piles and the coconut that was left over—you guessed it—they gave to the monkey.

What is the smallest number of coconuts they could have started with?

puzzle 78

A clerk was asked to do a mailing to a 10% sample of a company's clients. From the full mailing list, the clerk decided to pick the first client, skip one, pick the next, skip two, pick the next, skip three, pick the next, and so on, until he came to the end of the list. To his surprise, the final client that he picked happened to be the last one on the mailing list and, as required, he had then picked exactly 10% of the total.

How many names were on the mailing list?

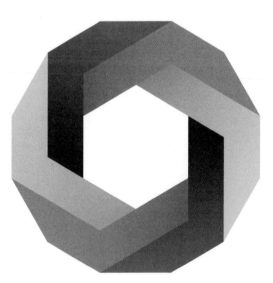

puzzle 79

The pattern below was made from two sets of 28 dominoes from which seven doubles (0-0, 1-1, 2-2, etc) are missing. The other seven doubles, all different, are either all placed vertically in the pattern or are all placed horizontally.

4	2	1	1	6	3
0	2	0	4	6	3
	6	3	2	6	
	1	3	3	5	
0	0	3	1	5	1
6	4	2	5	6	6

4	4	3	2	4	1
6	3	5	5	2	1
	2	4	2	2	
	3	4	6	1	
2	4	6	0	1	0
0	1	1	5	5	0

4	6			0	4
5	6	2	3	5	4
4	3	3	1	0	6
4	1	0	1	5	5
2	5	0	2	3	0
3	5	5	2	6	0

Identify the individual dominoes in the pattern.

Horizontal Dominoes						
0-1	0-2	0-3	0-4	0-5	0-6	1-2
1-3	1-4	1-5	1-6	2-3	2-4	2-5
2-6	3-4	3-5	3-6	4-5	4-6	5-6

Dominoes that are either Horizontal or Vertical						
0-0	1-1	2-2	3-3	4-4	5-5	6-6

Vertical Dominoes						
0 1	0 2	0 3	0 4	0 5	0 6	1 2
1 3	1 4	1 5	1 6	2 3	2 4	2 5
2 6	3 4	3 5	3 6	4 5	4 6	5 6

puzzle 6o

A man and a car pull up outside of a hotel and immediately go bankrupt. What has happened?

puzzle 6i

Without using a calculator, which is bigger: π^e or e^π?

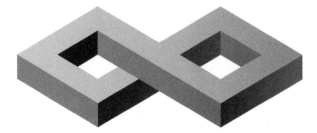

puzzle 82

This puzzle was composed by Hans August and Dr. Karl Fabel, and was published in 1949 in *Romana de Sah.* White has just made his seventeenth move.

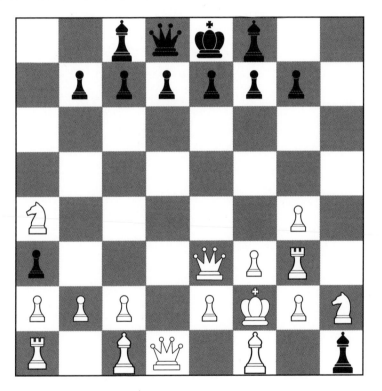

What was Black's ninth move, and what were the moves that followed it?

puzzle 63

A, B and C are standing in line, with B standing behind A and C standing behind B. Thus A cannot see B or C; B can see A, but cannot see C; C can see A and B. Each knows, and knows that the others know, that they are all experts in logic.

They are told there are five hats in total, three black and two white. Each then has one of the hats placed on their head from behind (so they cannot see the hat being put on their head).

> ➤ C says he doesn't know if his hat is black.

> ➤ B says she doesn't know if her hat is black.

> ➤ A then says that she knows whether her hat is black.

Is A's hat black?

puzzle 84

There is no trick to this question, but the answer can be expressed in an amusing way. What is the volume of a pizza of radius z and depth a?

puzzle 85

Here's one for people who know about the powers of mathematics. What is the next term in this series?

3   14   39   84   155   ?

puzzle 66

There are three jugs with capacities of 11, 13 and 17 cups. Each jug contains 9 cups of water. By pouring from jug to jug (and not spilling any water), how can you measure exactly 8 cups of water? There is more than one solution.

puzzle 67

What is the next term in this series?

100 121 144 202 244 400 ...

puzzle 88

A businessman usually travels home each evening on the same train, which is always on time, and his partner leaves home by car just in time to collect him from the station. One day the businessman caught an earlier train, and having forgotten to let his partner know, he walked to meet his partner's car and was then driven straight home, arriving ten minutes earlier than normal.

The businessman's partner always drives at a steady 36 mph each way. Had his partner been a faster driver, always averaging 46 mph each way, then they would have arrived home eight minutes earlier rather than ten.

How much earlier did the train arrive compared to the train that the businessman normally caught?

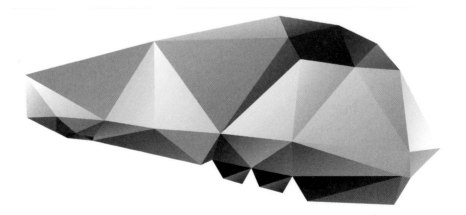

puzzle 89

Find three different two-digit primes where the average of any two is a prime, and the average of all three is a prime.

○ ○ ◍ ◐ ◍ ○ ○

puzzle 90

Using each of the digits 1, 5, 6 and 7 once and once only, brackets as required, and the symbols for addition, subtraction, multiplication and division as needed, find an expression that equals 21.

puzzle 91

A man decreed in his will that $240,000 should be divided equally among the cats and dogs he owns at the time of his death. When he died, the dogs in total received the same amount as the cats, and each animal who benefitted from the will received exactly $56,000 more than each of the man's cats and dogs would have received if the man had died immediately after writing his will.

How many cats and dogs did the man own when he wrote his will?

puzzle 92

P and Q are integers that between them contain each of the digits from 0 to 9 once and once only. What is the maximum value of P x Q?

○ ○ ◍ ◐ ◍ ○ ○

puzzle 93

S and T are integers that between them contain each of the digits from 0 to 9 once and once only. What is the minimum difference between S and T?

puzzle 94

This happy dog has his tail in the air and is looking left.
Move two matches so he still has his tail in the air, but is now
looking right.

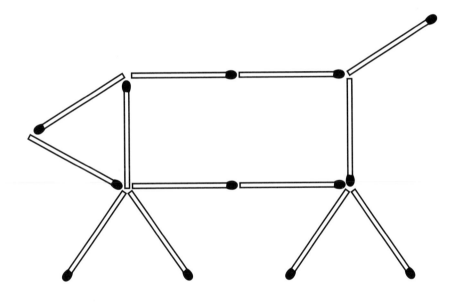

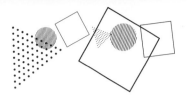

puzzle 95

Is the tenth root of ten
A little bit more
Than the root of the square
Of the sixth root of four?

○ ○ ◗ ◖ ◗ ○ ○

puzzle 96

This may seem self-contradictory, but find three integers in arithmetic progression (that is, with equal differences, such as 230, 236 and 242) whose product is prime.

puzzle 97

What is the smallest rectangle, by area, that can be divided exactly into five rectangles such that no two pairs of sides, including the sides of the original rectangle, have the same length, and the length of every side is a whole number of units?

---

puzzle 98

Without using a calculator or computer, can you find two integers whose squares add up to exactly 1,419,857? As a hint, the only prime factor for this number is 17.

puzzLe 99

The local kindergarten is thinking of making posters that show all the different ways of adding together two or more integers from 1 to 9 to make 10. For instance: 1 + 9 = 10, 9 + 1 = 10, 2 + 8 = 10, 8 + 2 = 10, and 2 + 1 + 2 + 1 + 1 + 2 + 1 = 10. Sums that contain the same numbers but in a different order are considered to be different.

The kindergarten has wall space for ten large posters, and there will be space on each poster for up to 50 possible solutions. Is that enough space for the kindergarten to display every possible solution?

puzzle 100

A swimmer swims at a constant speed. The distance from the jetty to where her boat is moored would normally take the swimmer ten minutes to swim. However, because she has the current with her, she is able to swim from the jetty to her boat in exactly five minutes. How long would it take her to swim back?

puzzle 101

This puzzle by Sam Loyd was published in the *Holyoke Transcript* in 1876. That White should win is obvious. Not obvious is doing it in three moves.

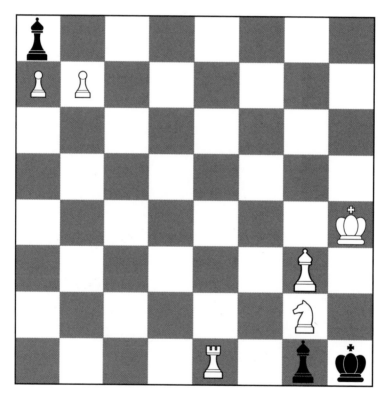

White to play and mate in three.

puzzle 102

An army four miles long steadily advances four miles while a dispatch rider gallops from the rear to the front, delivers a dispatch to the commanding general as he turns, and gallops back to the rear.

 How far has the rider journeyed?

puzzle 103

Using exactly four sixes and no other numbers, find an expression that is equal to 29. You may use brackets as required and as many of the symbols for addition, subtraction, multiplication, division, square root, decimal point, factorial and repeating decimals as required.

puzzle 104

Which is capable of filling more of the available space, a square peg in a round hole or a round peg in a square hole?

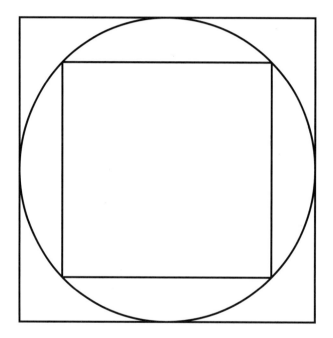

puzzle 105

The following six numbers can be grouped into three pairs such that the higher of each pair divided by the lower is a number (to an average of five decimal places) of particular mathematical significance.

113   323   355   408   577   878

What are the three pairs?

puzzLe 106

An expression for any integer between 0 and 64 can be made from exactly four threes using brackets as needed and the symbols for addition, subtraction, multiplication, division, square root, decimal point, factorial and repeating decimals as required. For example: 33 – 33 = 0.

Complete the table below. Three of the more challenging expressions to find are for the numbers 44, 47 and 49.

1		2	
3		4	
5		6	
7		8	
9		10	
11		12	
13		14	
15		16	
17		18	
19		20	
21		22	
23		24	

25		26	
27		28	
29		30	
31		32	
33		34	
35		36	
37		38	
39		40	
41		42	
43		44	
45		46	
47		48	
49		50	
51		52	
53		54	
55		56	
57		58	
59		60	
61		62	
63		64	

puzzle 107

A ladder 5m long leans against a wall. A cube measuring 1 x 1 x 1m just fits in the gap. If the base of the ladder is nearer to the wall than the top of the ladder is to the ground, how far is the base of the ladder from the wall?

puzzle 108

What is the smallest number that leaves a remainder of 1 when divided by 2, a remainder of 2 when divided by 3, a remainder of 3 when divided by 4, and so on up to a remainder of 17 when divided by 18?

puzzle 109

Over several soccer seasons, each of the eleven players had scored a prime number of goals, and the team's average was also a prime number. Nobody scored more than 45 goals, no player's tally was the same as the team average, and no two players had scored the same number of goals.

How many goals had each player scored?

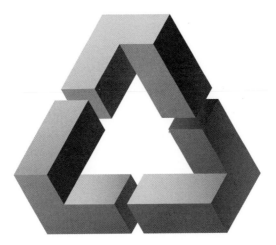

puzzle 110

The pattern below is made from a full set of dominoes plus one extra domino, and that domino is a double (e.g., 0-0, 1-1, 2-2, etc). If put together, the two numbers blanked out in the top two corners of the pattern would make that double.

	1	2	2	4	1	0	
4	1	4	5	5	2	6	6
0	2	4			6	1	0
5	0	1			5	6	0
6	5	4	3	2	1	3	3
3	3	1			5	2	1
		3	3	6	0		
		5	2	0	6		
		5	2	4	6		
		3	0	4	4		

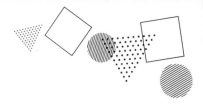

What are the blanked-out numbers?

To help you, a full set of dominoes looks like this						
0-0	0-1	0-2	0-3	0-4	0-5	0-6
1-1	1-2	1-3	1-4	1-5	1-6	2-2
2-3	2-4	2-5	2-6	3-3	3-4	3-5
3-6	4-4	4-5	4-6	5-5	5-6	6-6

puzzLe III

The magic square below has a hole in the middle and uses 24 dominoes from a set of 28 dominoes. Before eight numbers were blanked out, the numbers in each row and each column added to 19.

6	2	2	2	0	5	2
	3		3	4	2	4
5	5	3	1			4
3	4	3		4	5	0
1	1	6	5			6
	4		5	4	1	3
2	0	2	3	6	6	0

The blanked-out numbers combined with the numbers on the four missing dominoes are:

0, 0, 0, 0, 1, 1, 1, 1, 2, 3, 4, 5, 5, 6, 6 and 6

Identify the position of each domino in the magic square and name the missing dominoes.

To help you, a full set of dominoes looks like this						
0-0	0-1	0-2	0-3	0-4	0-5	0-6
1-1	1-2	1-3	1-4	1-5	1-6	2-2
2-3	2-4	2-5	2-6	3-3	3-4	3-5
3-6	4-4	4-5	4-6	5-5	5-6	6-6

puzzle 112

Find a ten-digit number containing each digit once where the number formed by the first 2 digits is divisible by 2, the number formed by the first 3 digits is divisible by 3, the number formed by the first 4 digits is divisible by 4, and so on.

puzzle 113

A box contains 13 lemons and 15 oranges. There are another 15 oranges outside the box.

Two pieces of fruit are removed from the box. If they are the same, then an orange is added to the box. If they are not the same, then a lemon is added to the box.

If this process continues until there is only one piece of fruit left in the box, what will it be?

puzzle 114

Two passengers set out at the same time to travel opposite ways around a circular railway during daylight. Clockwise trains take two hours for the journey, counterclockwise trains take three hours. Trains start each way every 15 minutes.

Including trains seen at the starting point and the ones they are on, how many trains did each passenger see on their journey?

○ ○ ◉ ◐ ◉ ○ ○

puzzle 115

I'm thinking of four positive integers that total less than 18 that are different from each other. If I just told you their product you would not be able to identify the four integers, but if I also told you the smallest of the four integers you could. But you don't know their product and you don't know what the smallest integer is . . . or do you?

puzzle 116

Three children of different ages share the same birthday. On one of their birthdays, one of their ages was the sum of the other two ages. On another birthday a few years later, the youngest observed that one of their ages was half the sum of the other two ages. When the number of years since the first occasion was half the sum of the ages on the first occasion, one celebrated her 18th birthday. What birthdays were the other two celebrating at this time?

puzzle 117

Find two ten-digit numbers, each containing the digits from 0 to 9 once and once only, with the property that successive pairs of digits, from left to right, are divisible in turn by 2, 3, 4, 5, 6, 7, 8, 9 and 10.

puzzle 118

What is the next term in this series:

1248   1632   6412   8256   ?

puzzLe 119

Three integers between 1 and 5 are chosen at random. P is told their product and S is told their sum. P and S know each other to be expert logicians and converse as follows:

a) P says to S that he doesn't know her sum.

b) S says to P that she doesn't know his product.

c) P says to S again that he doesn't know her sum.

d) S says to P again that she doesn't know his product.

e) P for the third time says to S that he doesn't know her sum.

f) S says to P that she now knows what the three integers are.

What is the product of the three integers?

puzzle 120

The final of the Tiddlywinks Club Championship features two players: Tiddle and Wink. Both players know that in any one game between them, Tiddle has a two out of three chance of winning.

The championship is a best-of-nine series. Tiddle says that, according to the odds, after six games the score should be 4-2 to him, but to save time, he'd be willing to start the championship from a base score of 3-2 to him, thereby leaving Wink a chance of being tied 3-3 after game six.

Wink would like to give himself the best chance of winning the championship. Should he accept Tiddle's offer?

puzzLe 121

A right-angle triangle has an area of 666,666. No side of this triangle shares a common factor with another side or is smaller than 666. What is the length of the triangle's hypotenuse?

○ ○ ◑ ◐ ◑ ○ ○

puzzLe 122

With a single stroke of the pen made to the left of the equal sign, make this equation true:

5 + 5 + 5 = 550

puzzle 123

A total of five triangles can be identified in the diagram on the left.

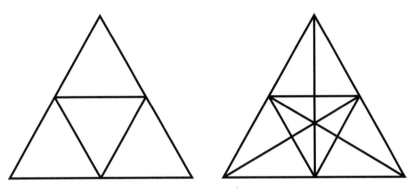

How many triangles are there in the diagram on the right?

puzzle 124

The magic square below has a hole in the middle and uses 24 dominoes from a set of 28 dominoes. Before ten numbers were blanked out, the numbers in each row and each column added to 22.

3	4		4	6	2	
5	4	3	1	1	4	4
	2		6	6	3	3
2	1		■	3	6	
	6		3	1	0	1
6	5	1	4	3	2	1
1	0		4	2	5	

The blanked-out numbers combined with the numbers on the four missing dominoes are:

0, 0, 0, 0, 0, 0, 2, 2, 2, 3, 4, 5, 5, 5, 5, 5, 6 and 6.

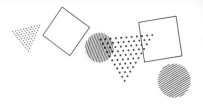

Identify the position of each domino in the magic square and name the missing dominoes.

To help you, a full set of dominoes looks like this						
0-0	0-1	0-2	0-3	0-4	0-5	0-6
1-1	1-2	1-3	1-4	1-5	1-6	2-2
2-3	2-4	2-5	2-6	3-3	3-4	3-5
3-6	4-4	4-5	4-6	5-5	5-6	6-6

puzzle 125

In the expression below, must the three letters A, N and E represent three different digits?

$$(ANNE)_{\text{base 8}} - (ANNE)_{\text{base 5}} = (ANNE)_{\text{base 7}}$$

○ ○ ◐ ◑ ◐ ○ ○

puzzle 126

In a league of four hockey teams, each team played the other three. After all six games had been played, the following league table was prepared:

Team	Goals	
	For	Against
A	4	0
B	2	1
C	1	3
D	2	5

Team D drew one game and lost its other two. What was the score in each of the six games?

puzzle 127

Two candles were lit. The longer and thinner one was lit at 4pm and the shorter but fatter one 15 minutes later. Each candle burned at a steady rate, and by 8pm both were the same length. The thinner candle, which initially was 2 cm longer than the fatter one, burned out at midnight and the fatter one an hour later. How long was each candle originally?

puzzle 128

In the game of bridge, hands are commonly assessed by assigning points to the high cards using the system below, and then adding up the points:

- ➤ 4 points for an ace

- ➤ 3 points for a king

- ➤ 2 points for a queen

- ➤ 1 point for a jack

It is possible for a partnership that between them holds just five points to make a grand slam (all 13 tricks) against any defence. Find an example of such a hand.

puzzle 129

Taika and his son Tane are in the garden planting kumara runners. Orange kumara for one plot, red kumara for another plot, and an even mixture of both for the middle plot.

To ensure that the correct runners are used, Taika and Tane only take runners for one plot at a time. The number of runners they take can be anything from one upwards. If the runners are for the middle plot, they make sure they have the same number of each type.

It has been a long day, and all that remains to be planted is 18 orange kumara runners and 11 red kumara runners. Taika is pleased with his son's work, and offers to double his allowance if, by taking turns removing the remaining runners for planting as described above, Tane plants the last runner.

If Tane has the choice of planting the next batch or letting his father go first, which should he choose to ensure that he is able to double his allowance?

puzzle 130

There was a group of three goblins. When asked a question, one of the goblins would always answer truthfully, one would always lie, and the third would lie at random. They know who has which habit, but you do not.

How—in only three questions, to which the goblin being asked can answer only "yes" or "no"—can you discover which goblin has which habit? Each of the three questions can be put to one goblin only, but it doesn't need to be to the same goblin each time. For example, questions one and two could go to the first goblin, and question three to the second.

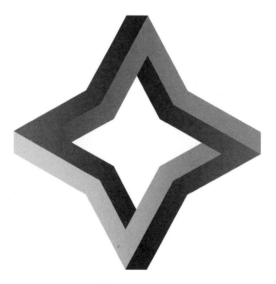

puzzle 131

Three people weighing 72 pounds, 84 pounds and 156 pounds, and a weight of 60 pounds, are on top of a tower. A pulley is fixed to the top of the tower, and running over the pulley is a rope with a basket at each end.

The baskets are only big enough to hold two people, or one person and the weight. There are no restrictions on operating the pulley with the baskets empty or with just the weight, but for safety's sake there cannot be more than a 12-pound difference in weight between the two baskets if either basket is carrying a person.

How can the three use the pulley and the baskets to get themselves and the weight down from the tower?

puzzle 132

The pattern below is made from two sets of dominoes. Dominoes from one set are positioned in the puzzle horizontally, and dominoes from the other set are positioned vertically.

Box 1

4	6	0	0	0	1
1	5	0	2	2	6
5	0	1	1	6	3
3	6	1	5	0	0
4	4	6	3	5	3
6	2	6	4	2	6

Box 2

2	0	5	6	1	3
3	2	4	2	5	2
3	6	1	2	3	3
4	1	5	5	0	5
0	2	6	1	6	4
5	3	4	3	5	4

5	0	1	2	5	4
1	2	3	0	5	3
6	0	6	1	1	0
4	1	5	0	2	4
2	4	3	4	5	4
3	2	4	0	2	3

Box 3

Box 4

The dominoes blanked out in Box 4 are a double 1 and a double 6. Were they placed vertically or horizontally?

Vertical Dominoes						
0 0	0 1	0 2	0 3	0 4	0 5	0 6
1 1	1 2	1 3	1 4	1 5	1 6	2 2
2 3	2 4	2 5	2 6	3 3	3 4	3 5
3 6	4 4	4 5	4 6	5 5	5 6	6 6

Horizontal Dominoes						
0-0	0-1	0-2	0-3	0-4	0-5	0-6
1-1	1-2	1-3	1-4	1-5	1-6	2-2
2-3	2-4	2-5	2-6	3-3	3-4	3-5
3-6	4-4	4-5	4-6	5-5	5-6	6-6

puzzle 133

Just by guessing (and using some inspiration!), can you find the square root of this number?

12,345,678,987,654,321

○ ○ ◑ ◐ ◑ ○ ○

puzzle 134

What is the missing number?

9 22 24 12 ? 4 13

puzzle 135

In the land of Anything Is Possible, B946 and Q142 set off for a walk with their dog, Spot. B946 walks at 6 km per hour, Q142 walks at 5 km per hour, and Spot runs from one to the other at 8 km per hour, turning instantaneously when required.

Where is Spot relative to B946 and Q142 after thirty minutes?

puzzle 136

In 1998, the U.K. Institute of Actuaries celebrated its 150th anniversary. At that time, a puzzle was proposed that asked for each of the integers from 1 to 150 to be made using only the digits 1, 9, 9 and 8; parentheses as required; and the mathematical symbols for addition, subtraction, multiplication, division, factorial, decimal point and repeating decimal as required.

The number that eluded most would-be solvers was 148. It is not easy to find, but there is a solution for this number as well. What is it?

puzzle 137

Two pupils were to be chosen at random from a school register to take part in a competition. The probability that both would be boys was one-third. Before the choice could be made, however, a decision was made to include pupils from the register of another school in the drawing for the two places. This other school had a register of 1,000 pupils, and the chance that the two selected pupils would both be boys was reduced to one-thirteenth.

How many pupils are on the register of the first school?

puzzle 138

The rectangular doorway to a giraffe house is higher than it is wide, and its height and width both measure an integral number of feet. The area of the doorway in square feet is 25% greater than the doorway's perimeter.

What is the height of the doorway?

puzzle 139

What property having to do with fourth powers do the three numbers below have in common?

1634 8208 9474

○ ○ ◑ ◐ ◑ ○ ○
---

puzzle 140

Prime Palace (see Puzzle 38) now wants to move to a six-figure system. Will there be a suitable new bracelet for the king?

puzzle 141

In a game of chess, Black has agreed to mirror White's first three moves. White promptly mates Black on her fourth move. What were White's moves?

--- ○ ○ ◑ ◐ ◑ ○ ○ ---

puzzle 142

A right triangle measuring 5 x 12 x 13 has an area (in square units) equal to its perimeter (in units). Name another right triangle with integral measurements that has this property.

puzzle 143

In this crossnumber puzzle, each number to be entered in the diagram is clued by the number of factors it has. In this context, both 1 and the number itself are counted as factors. For example, if 14 were one of the numbers to be entered in the diagram, its clue would be 4, since 14 for the purposes of this puzzle has four factors (1, 2, 7 and 14).

No answer begins with a zero, and in the finished diagram, each of the digits from 0 to 9 must appear twice.

Across

1. 8
2. 12
4. 2
6. 6
8. 6
9. 24
10. 14
11. 6

Down

1. 15
2. 2
3. 9
5. 18
7. 8
9. 10

puzzle 144

Imagine a clock face that has no numerals for the hour markings, just dots. At each hour on the hour the reflection of the clock will show a correct time reading (it does not matter whether it is the actual time). How many other times in a period of twelve hours does this happen?

puzzle 145

On a board displaying the hymn numbers to be sung, each number was a three-digit prime and each of the digits from 1 to 9 appeared just once.

The sum of the hymns' numbers was less than 1,000. What were the numbers of the hymns?

puzzle 146

An expression for any integer between 0 and 112 can be made from exactly four fours using brackets as needed and the symbols for addition, subtraction, multiplication, division, square root, decimal point, factorial and repeating decimals as required. However, all that is asked for here are expressions for 73 and 89—but they are not easy.

○ ○ ◑ ◐ ◑ ○ ○

puzzle 147

The third and fourth powers of this integer contain between them exactly one of each digit. What is the integer?

puzzle 148

In a game of table tennis, 24 of the 37 points played were won by the player serving, and Smith beat Jones 21-16. Remembering that, in table tennis, service alternates every five points, who served first?

puzzle 149

A car is parked on a steep hill when the brakes suddenly fail. In the first second, the car rolls 12 inches. Assuming constant acceleration, how far will it have rolled after five seconds?

puzzle 150

The pattern below is made from two sets of dominoes. Dominoes from one set are positioned in the puzzle horizontally, and dominoes from the other set are positioned vertically.

Box 1

6	6	1	5	6	2	1
2	5	3	1	0	0	4
5	3	1	0	4	4	5
0	2	6	4	6	3	3

Box 2

0	1	0	2	4	0	0
4	3	2	3	4	1	3
4	0	4	1	1	1	6
1	2	5	6	5	1	3

1	3	6	0	6	2	5
1	5	5	0	4	2	2
6	0	4	5	2	4	4
3	0	6	6	2	0	5

Box 3

2	5	3	5	4	1	6
1	5	6	5	3	3	6
2	3	2	5	3	4	6
4	3	1	0	0	2	2

Box 4

In one of the four boxes above, all the dominoes are positioned vertically. Identify the position of each domino.

Horizontal Dominoes

0-0	0-1	0-2	0-3	0-4	0-5	0-6
1-1	1-2	1-3	1-4	1-5	1-6	2-2
2-3	2-4	2-5	2-6	3-3	3-4	3-5
3-6	4-4	4-5	4-6	5-5	5-6	6-6

Vertical Dominoes

0 0	0 1	0 2	0 3	0 4	0 5	0 6
1 1	1 2	1 3	1 4	1 5	1 6	2 2
2 3	2 4	2 5	2 6	3 3	3 4	3 5
3 6	4 4	4 5	4 6	5 5	5 6	6 6

puzzLe ı5ı

Which five of these six pieces can be arranged to form a 5 x 5 checkerboard pattern?

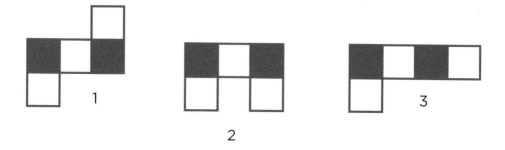

1

2

3

4

5

6

puzzle 152

If B is two A,
C three A plus B,
And A is "eleven eleven,"
Is B to the C
Plus C to the B
Divisible by seven?

"Eleven eleven,"
So you won't be confused,
Has nothing to do with odd bases.
It's simply ten thou
That's multiplied by
One ninth to four decimal places.

puzzle 153

There are several ways in which 16 dots can be placed in 16 different squares in an 8 x 8 array such that every row, column and diagonal (not just the main diagonals) is either empty or has exactly two dots in it. The solution shown below is one such arrangement, and in this case it is symmetrical when divided in half diagonally from top left to bottom right.

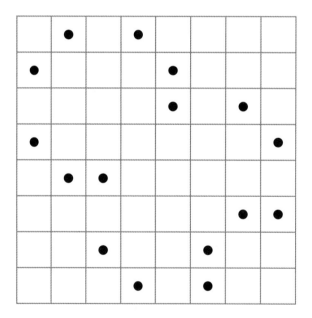

Find a solution that is not symmetrical.

puzzle 154

With a single stroke of the pen made left of the equal sign, make this equation true:

$$10\ 10\ 10 = 9.50$$

puzzle 155

The ages of Old and Young total 48. Old is twice as old as Young was when Old was half as old as Young will be when Young is three times as old as Old was when Old was three times as old as Young. How old is Old?

puzzle 156

Before the rugby season started, four players weighed in at 105, 110, 115 and 120 kg, respectively. At that time, Christian announced that he was going on a diet, and the other three decided to join him.

At the most recent weigh-in, no man's weight had changed by more than 5 kg, and all weights were still whole numbers of kilograms. Dan had lost more weight than Mr. Fitzpatrick. Ardie weighed 10 kg more than Dan when they started the diet. Mr. McCaw now weighs 10 kg less than Mr. Umaga. Mr. Lomu now weighs 7 kg less than Beauden did before dieting. Mr. Umaga actually put on weight, but still weighs less than Ardie. Beauden has lost more weight than Ardie. Mr. Fitzpatrick now weighs 4 kg more than Ardie.

What are the names and the new weights of the four players?

puzzle 157

Six people sit down to play a game of Cluedo/Clue, and then realize that the board has been mislaid. Undeterred, they still have the Cluedo cards, they agree that each player will simply take turns making a suggestion (or, in due course, an accusation), and that any room can be chosen each time.

A quick refresher on the rules. One character (out of six), one weapon (out of six), and one room card (out of nine) are set aside, and the rest of the cards are dealt out. With six players, this means that everyone receives three cards. When a suggestion is made, the next player must disprove it if they can, and if they cannot, then the player after them must disprove it if they can, and so on.

You are player A, and deal yourself Miss Scarlett, the Revolver, and the Ballroom. The game then progresses with players making the following suggestions:

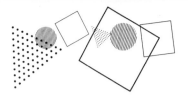

Player	Character	Weapon	Room	DB*
B	Col. Mustard	Dagger	Billiard Room	E
C	Prof. Plum	Lead Pipe	Study	E
D	Mrs. White	Wrench	Conservatory	F
E	Mr. Green	Wrench	Library	F
F	Mrs. Peacock	Revolver	Hall	A
A	Mr. Green	Candlestick	Dining Room	F
B	Mrs. Peacock	Rope	Ballroom	E
C	Col. Mustard	Wrench	Lounge	B
D	Prof. Plum	Dagger	Kitchen	B
E	Prof. Plum	Lead Pipe	Study	B
F	Mrs. White	Lead Pipe	Conservatory	E

Disproved by

Player F then disproves your suggestion of Mr. Green with the Candlestick in the Dining Room by showing you the Dining Room. What is the winning accusation?

puzzle 158

Two brothers go shopping for a birthday present. Eventually they find a nice vase and, paying half each, they pay the shopkeeper £20.

Shortly after the brothers have left the shop, the shopkeeper realizes that the price of the vase should have been £17. He is an honest man, and sends his assistant after the brothers with a refund of £3.

The shopkeeper's assistant is not so honest, and instead of refunding the brothers £3 gives the brothers just £1 each, keeping £1 for himself.

On returning to the shop the assistant is feeling guilty and wants to confess to the shopkeeper what he has done, but now he is totally confused. The brothers paid £9 each (£10 each less the £1 refund) and he has the £1 he kept, making a total of £19, not £20.

He can feel the £1 he stole in his pocket. Where did the other £1 go?

puzzle 159

There are five men in five houses. Each man comes from a different town (all genuine names), has a different pet and supports a different rugby team. From the following clues, determine which man supports the Waratahs and, if different, which man has a kea.

> ➤ The five houses are in a row and each is a different hue.

> ➤ The man who has the kangaroo lives next to the man from Woy Woy.

> ➤ Mr. Brown supports the Brumbies.

> ➤ The man from Wagga Wagga lives in the blue house.

> ➤ Mr. Green lives in the mauve house.

> ➤ The man from Bong Bong has a kookaburra.

> ➤ Mr. White comes from Aka Aka.

> ➤ Mr. Gray lives on the left in the first house.

> ➤ The red house is to the right of and adjacent to the yellow house.

- The man from Peka Peka supports the Hurricanes.

- The man who has a koala lives next door to the man from Wagga Wagga.

- Mr. Black has a kiwi.

- The man in the middle house supports the Rebels.

- The man in the red house supports the Crusaders.

- The maroon house is next to Mr. Gray's house.

puzzle 160

This puzzle and illustration have been taken from *The Canterbury Puzzles and Other Curious Problems* by Henry Ernest Dudeney, which was first published in 1907.

The Miller next took the company aside and showed them nine sacks of flour that were standing as depicted in the sketch. "Now, hearken, all and some," said he, "while that I do set ye the riddle of the nine sacks of flour. And mark ye, my lords and masters, that there be single sacks on the outside, pairs next unto them, and three together in the middle thereof. By Saint Benedict, it doth so happen that if we do but multiply the pair, 28, by the single one, 7, the answer is 196, which is of a truth the number shown by the sacks in the middle. Yet it be not true that the other pair, 34, when so multiplied by its neighbour, 5, will also make 196.

Wherefore I do beg you, gentle sirs, so to place anew the nine sacks with as little trouble as possible that each pair when thus multiplied by its single neighbour shall make the number in the middle." As the Miller has stipulated in effect that as few bags as possible shall be moved, there is only one answer to this puzzle, which everybody should be able to solve.

Few would disagree that H. E. Dudeney (1857-1930) is England's puzzle master.

puzzle 161

No answer begins with a zero.

1	2	3	4	5	6	7
8			9			
10				11		12
13		14			15	
16	17		18	19		
20				21		
22					23	

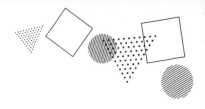

Across

1. See 3-Down
3. A multiple of 3
8. 3 x 17-Down
9. 2 x 15-Down
10. See 14-Down
11. See 6-Down
13. 2 x 4-Down
16. Not 3-Down
18. See 5-Down
20. 2 x 2-Down
21. Not 6-Down
22. See 1-Down
23. Same as 20-Down

Down

1. 2 x 22-Across
2. See 20-Across
3. 2 x 1-Across
4. See 13-Across
5. 2 x 18-Across
6. 3 x 11-Across
7. Same as 23-Across
12. 2 x 3-Across
14. 2 x 10-Across + 4
15. See 9-Across
17. See 8-Across
19. Square of 23-Across
20. See 23-Across

puzzle 1

2,100,010,006.

puzzle 2

Although gravity is lower on the moon than on Earth, helicopters cannot fly on the moon as there is no atmosphere for them to fly in.

puzzle 3

3-5 is in row 1, so 2-7 is somewhere in row 2. Therefore, 1-2 is in row 5 and 3-7 in row 1. Missing dominoes: 1-5, 1-6, 2-5 and 4-4.

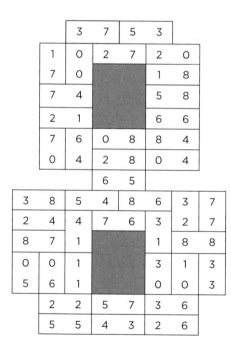

puzzle 4

The missing numbers in rows 3, 4 and 5 are 1, 5, 4 and 2. Row 2, column 2 must be a 0. Row 1, column 1 must be a 3. Missing dominoes: 0-1, 1-1, 3-5 and 4-6.

3	6	1	5	3	0	3
1	0	2	5	3	4	6
2	6	2	1	3	1	6
4	3	5		4	2	3
5	6	0	2	4	4	0
2	0	6	2	4	5	2
4	0	5	6	0	5	1

puzzle 5

The answer is none. This is because after 100 laps there will only be ten treasure chests with their lids open. They are: 1, 4, 9, 16, 25, 36, 49, 64, 81 and 100. Each of these numbers is a perfect square, meaning it is equal to a whole number multiplied by itself. Because perfect squares, by definition, can always be factorized as a number multiplied by itself, perfect squares (and only perfect squares) always have an odd number of factors. Thus their lids end up open and the rest of the lids end up shut.

puzzle 6

Q is 67,980, and 54,321 x 67,980 = 3,692,741,580.

puzzle 7

The distances between the refreshment stations are 1, 3, 2, 7, 8 and 10 miles.

puzzle 8

Eleven students passed Exam One only, three passed Exam Two only, and eight passed Exam Three only. Thus ten students (= 32 – 11 – 3 – 8) passed more than one exam. One of the keys to solving this puzzle is recognizing the requirement for the answers to be whole numbers.

puzzle 9

True. It is not possible to end up with just one peg on the board if the central hole starts off empty. To show this, label the holes and the pegs that are in those holes as shown:

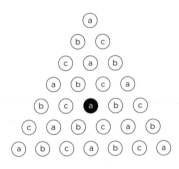

Initially there are nine pegs of each letter. After any move, the number of pegs in two of a, b and c will be reduced by one, and the number of pegs in the holes of the remaining letter will be increased by one. Thus, at any stage, the amount of pegs assigned to each letter will either be all odd or all even. Hence it is impossible to be left with only one peg on the board, for this would require an odd number (namely one) of pegs in holes of one particular letter and an even number (namely zero) of pegs in the holes of the two other letters.

The proof above is for when the central hole starts off empty, but the reasoning is equally valid whichever hole marked a starts off empty.

puzzle 10

Three planes are needed. The planes set off together and fly one eighth of the way around the world. One then tops up the other two with fuel before returning to base. The other two planes continue until they are a quarter of the way around the world, then one tops up the other with fuel and returns to base.

The remaining plane then flies solo until it is three quarters of the way around the world when the above operations are carried out in reverse: one plane meets the first plane at the three-quarter point and gives it a quarter tank of fuel; then the two planes fly to the seven-eighths point, where they are met by the third plane, which gives them each another quarter tank of fuel. All three planes then have enough fuel to get them to base.

puzzle 11

Hassan has a 2% chance of getting a special meal; Susie is certain of getting a special meal. For Susie there are two possibilities:

i. If Hassan sat in a "special-meal seat," then the next 98 people will sit in their allocated seats, leaving the second "special-meal seat" free for Susie.

ii. If Hassan did not sit in a "special-meal seat," then eventually one of the next 98 boarding passengers will sit in one of the two "special-meal seats," which means that any remaining "normal-meal seat" passengers will sit in their allocated seats. Susie then sits in the other "special-meal seat."

puzzle 12

There were 6 + 7 = 13 games where the player who threw first went on to win the game, so there were 25 – 13 = 12 games where the player who went first ended up losing the game.

The order of play for the next game changes when a player who went first loses the game. Given that Joe threw first in the first game and that there were an even number of games (12) where the player who threw first lost the game, it follows that Joe would have thrown first had there been a 26th game. Joe must therefore have won the 25th game and the tournament.

puzzle 13

72 hens, 21 sheep, 7 cows.

puzzle 14

The statements can be rewritten as follows:

➢ Today is Thursday.
➢ Today is Tuesday.
➢ Today is Sunday.
➢ Today is Sunday, Monday, Tuesday, Wednesday, Thursday or Friday.

- ➢ Today is Tuesday.
- ➢ Today is Wednesday, Thursday, Friday or Saturday.
- ➢ Today is Monday.

The only day that is not mentioned more than once is Saturday, so today must be Saturday.

puzzle 15

Each line describes the line above. For example, line five is 1 1 1 2 2 1, which can be expressed as three ones (3 1), two twos (2 2) and one one (1 1), so line six is 3 1 2 2 1 1. The ninth line in the pyramid is: 3 1 1 3 1 2 1 1 1 3 1 2 2 1.

puzzle 16

A solution for zero is 44 − 44. For the integers 1 to 10:

$1 = 44 \div 44$ $2 = (4 \div 4) + (4 \div 4)$
$3 = (4 + 4 + 4) \div 4$ $4 = 4 + ((4 - 4) \times 4)$
$5 = ((4 \times 4) + 4) \div 4$ $6 = 4 + ((4 + 4) \div 4)$
$7 = (44 \div 4) - 4$ $8 = 4 + 4 + 4 - 4$
$9 = 4 + 4 + (4 \div 4)$ $10 = (44 - 4) \div 4$

puzzle 17

$11 = 44 \div \sqrt{4} \div \sqrt{4}$ $12 = (44 + 4) \div 4$
$13 = (44 \div 4) + \sqrt{4}$ $14 = 4 + 4 + 4 + \sqrt{4}$
$15 = (44 \div 4) + 4$ $16 = 4 + 4 + 4 + 4$
$17 = (4 \times 4) + (4 \div 4)$ $18 = (4 \times 4) + (4 \div \sqrt{4})$
$19 = (4 + 4 - .4) \div .4$ $20 = (4 \div .4) + (4 \div .4)$
$21 = (44 - \sqrt{4}) \div \sqrt{4}$ $22 = (4 \times 4) + 4 + \sqrt{4}$
$23 = (44 + \sqrt{4}) \div \sqrt{4}$ $24 = (4 \times 4) + 4 + 4$
$25 = (\sqrt{4} \div .4) \times (\sqrt{4} \div .4)$ $26 = (44 \div \sqrt{4}) + 4$
$27 = (\sqrt{4} \div .4)^{\sqrt{4}} + \sqrt{4}$ $28 = 44 - (4 \times 4)$
$29 = (\sqrt{4} \div .4)^{\sqrt{4}} + 4$ $30 = (\sqrt{4} \div .4) \times (4 + \sqrt{4})$

puzzle 18

51983

puzzle 19

Missing dominoes:
0-5, 1-7, 2-4 and 5-5.

```
          6  4  2  7
       5  1  3  7  4  2
       8  0  ▓  ▓  0  0
       1  7  ▓  ▓  0  8
       8  5  ▓  ▓  4  8
       3  5  5  3  6  2
       8  4  7  4  5  8
             6  1
 6  2  8  7  2  5  6  8
 6  1  1  8  8  4  4  2
 7  4  6  ▓  ▓  3  1  3
 0  6  0  ▓  ▓  3  1  3
 0  1  1  ▓  ▓  0  0  3
       2  3  5  7  3  6
       2  4  2  6  7  7
```

puzzle 20

If Jill had said that the number was neither a perfect square nor a perfect cube, then Jack would not have had enough information for an answer. Therefore, Jill must have said that the number was a square or a cube or both. The table below shows the possibilities:

Range	Squares	Cubes	Both
13-499	16, 25, 36, 49, 64, 81, 100, 121, 144, 169, 196, 225, 256, 289, 324, 361, 400, 441, 484	27, 64, 125, 216, 343	64
500-1,300	529, 576, 625, 676, 729, 784, 841, 900, 961, 1,024, 1,089, 1,156, 1,225, 1,296	512, 729, 1,000	729

Jill could not have said that the number was a perfect square and a perfect cube; otherwise, Jack could have guessed the number after three questions.

If Jill had said that the number was a perfect square but not a perfect cube, then the fourth question would not have been sufficient to identify the number.

If Jill had said that the number was a perfect cube but not a perfect square, then the fourth question would have been sufficient to identify the number (512 or 1,000) only if Jill had said that the number was not below 500.

Jill therefore answered that the number was not below 500, was not a perfect square, but was a perfect cube. This tells us that the number is below 500, is a perfect square, and is a perfect cube. Therefore, Jill's number is 64.

puzzle 21

Since the first person could not determine the hue of the ball in box 2, boxes 1 and 3 must have contained red/yellow, yellow/red or red/red. (If they had contained yellow/yellow, he would have known box 2 contained a red ball.)

If box 3 had contained a yellow ball, the second person would have been able to determine that box 1 contained a red ball. Since he could not do so, box 3 must contain a red ball.

puzzle 22

There were eight people at the meeting before the new person arrived, for a total of 28 handshakes. The new person knew seven of the eight other people at the meeting.

puzzle 23

Prime numbers of more than one digit end with 1, 3, 7 or 9, as do numbers that are three times prime numbers of more than one digit. Neither the third nor the sixth digit of the required ten-digit number can be 7, and 9 cannot appear anywhere in the number. Knowing these facts narrows down the possibilities. The required number is 2,412,134,003.

puzzle 24

NAME	CITY	LAST DINNER	NEXT DINNER
Anouk	Auckland	Wholemeal Cafe	Farewell Spit Cafe
Bosai	Dunedin	Collingwood Tavern	The Old School Cafe
Carmen	Christchurch	Milliways Restaurant	Wholemeal Cafe
Diego	Wellington	The Old School Cafe	Milliways Restaurant
Eduardo	Hamilton	Farewell Spit Cafe	Collingwood Tavern

puzzle 25

The only way that A could have immediately known what was on her hat is if the other two hats had had the same integer on them (as hers would then have been the sum of those two integers because it cannot be the difference, the difference being zero). She didn't know immediately, so we can eliminate a solution of the form (2n, n, n). From B's "no," and using the same logic, we eliminate (n, 2n, n), and knowing that B knows from A's answer that the solution isn't of the form (2n, n, n) we can also eliminate (2n, 3n, n).

C's "yes" means the solution is of the form (n, n, 2n), (2n, n, 3n), (n, 2n, 3n) or (2n, 3n, 5n). Because C's answer was 25, which is not divisible by 2 or 3, the solution must be of the form (2n, 3n, 5n). As C's integer was 25, then A's integer was 10 and B's integer was 15.

puzzle 26

Digital Root $(9^{6130} + 2)^{4875}$

= Digital Root $(2^{4875} + 9 \times (\text{large number}))$

= Digital Root $(8^{1625} + 9)$

= Digital Root $((9 - 1)^{1625} + 9)$

= Digital Root $((9 \times (\text{large number}) - 1) + 9)$

= Digital Root $(9 - 1 + 9)$

= 8

puzzle 27

1	9 – 5 – 3	2	5 – 3	3	3
4	7 – 3	5	5	6	9 – 3
7	7	8	5 + 3	9	9
10	7 + 3	11	9 + 5 – 3	12	9 + 3
13	9 + 7 – 3	14	9 + 5	15	7 + 5 + 3
16	9 + 7	17	9 + 5 + 3	18	(5 – 3) × 9
19	9 + 7 + 3	20	(9 × 3) – 7	21	7 × 3
22	(9 × 3) – 5	23	37 – 9 – 5	24	9 + 7 + 5 + 3
25	(7 × 3) + 9 – 5	26	35 – 9	27	9 × 3
28	(9 – 5) × 7	29	(7 × 5) + 3 – 9	30	(7 × 3) + 9
31	(5 × 3) + 9 + 7	32	37 – 5	33	37 + 5 – 9
34	39 – 5	35	35	36	(7 + 5) × 3
37	37	38	(7 × 5) + 3	39	39
40	(9 – 5) × (7 + 3)	41	37 + 9 – 5	42	35 + 7
43	3 × (9 + 7) – 5	44	35 + 9	45	9 × 5
46	37 + 9	47	(7 × 5) + 9 + 3	48	57 – 9
49	59 – 7 – 3	50	(7 + 3) × 5	51	35 + 9 + 7
52	59 – 7	53	53	54	57 – 3
55	59 + 3 – 7	56	59 – 3	57	57
58	95 – 37	59	59	60	53 + 7
61	(9 × 7) + 3 – 5	62	53 + 9	63	9 × 7
64	73 – 9	65	(9 × 7) + 5 – 3	66	57 + 9

67	5 x (9 + 3) + 7	68	73 – 5	69	53 + 9 + 7
70	35 x (9 – 7)	71	79 – 5 – 3	72	75 – 3
73	73	74	79 – 5	75	75
76	79 – 3	77	(9 + 5 – 3) x 7	78	73 + 5
79	79	80	(9 + 7) x 5	81	93 – 7 – 5
82	79 + 3	83	5 x (9 + 7) + 3	84	79 + 5
85	95 – 7 – 3	86	93 – 7	87	79 + 5 + 3
88	95 – 7	89	97 – 5 – 3	90	(7 + 3) x 9
91	95 + 3 – 7	92	95 – 3	93	93
94	97 – 3	95	95	96	59 + 37
97	97	98	95 + 3	99	95 + 7 – 3
100	93 + 7	101	7 x (9 + 5) + 3	102	97 + 5

puzzle 28

Ages	Sum	Third of Product
2, 3, 4	9	8
2, 3, 6	11	12
2, 2, 9	13	12
1, 6, 6	13	12
1, 6, 8	15	16
1, 4, 12	17	16
2, 2, 15	19	20
1, 4, 18	23	24

Let the children's ages be a, b and c, the number of their house be n, and the number of "the house next door" be m (so $m = n + 1$ or $m = n - 1$).

Without the correction, $abc = 3n$ and $a + b + c = n + 1$ or $n - 1$, and with the correction, $abc = 3m$ and $a + b + c = m + 1$ or $m - 1$.

At this stage it might seem that the equations are equivalent, and that the correction is a hoax, but read on! The table at left gives a complete list of three children's ages from which the sum of the ages differs by one from one third of their product.

In deciding which set of ages was most likely to be correct, the actuary must have assumed that the extra information regarding the eldest child having a paper round had been given for a reason, and that the reason was to distinguish between several possible answers for a given house number.

If the correction was a hoax (i.e., if the number of their house was a third of the product of their ages), then there are two possible house numbers, 12 and 16, for which extra information would have been required. If the correction was not a hoax, there is only one such house number, 13. As the actuary was "just about sure" that he had chosen the right ages, the correction was not a hoax.

puzzle 29

Let the width of the star be 2a, and construct a line from the central point of the star (and circle) to where one of the two outer threads meets the circle.

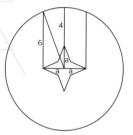

The radius of the circle is 4 + a. The diagonal line is a radius, but it is also the hypotenuse of a right-angled triangle with sides 6 and a. By the Pythagorean theorem we have $6^2 + a^2 = (4 + a)^2$, from which a = 2.5 cm and the width of the star is 5 cm.

puzzle 30

The two hands cannot occur in the same deal, so we compare the number of hands in each of those deals that beat these two.

They are both beaten by the same number of four-of-a-kinds, but the first hand is beaten by 32 straight flushes, the second by 31. Hence the full house with those three kings and two aces is the stronger hand.

puzzle 31

1	5	3	5	4	1	1
4	5	2	6	3	0	4
4	1	6	6	3	6	6
1	0	5	4	1	3	1

2	3	1	2	0	4	2
1	4	6	2	4	3	5
6	6	3	4	4	3	4
2	6	5	6	5	5	2

Either 2-6 vertical or 2-6 horizontal is in the lower left corner of the top right box. Therefore the corners of the bottom left box must be fives.

5	5	0	5	1	2	5
0	1	3	5	1	2	2
2	0	1	3	3	0	4
5	2	3	6	1	0	5

6	0	0	0	0	3	6
1	1	4	6	5	3	2
4	2	0	4	4	0	3
6	3	0	2	2	0	6

puzzle 32

Not eleven, but ten times. The times are between 1 and 2, between 2 and 3, and so on, ending with once between 10 and 11. It does not happen between 11 and 12, since it happens at exactly 12 (noon and midnight). The question excludes noon and midnight, so those occurrences don't count.

puzzle 33

The last-numbered page in the book is 141, and the missing leaf contains pages 5 and 6. The seemingly alternative solution of the last-numbered page being 142 and the missing leaf being pages 76 and 77 does not work. This is because page 76 would be on the left and page 77 on the right, and therefore on different leaves.

puzzle 34

puzzle 35

Assume for the first event there were B players from Bluetown and G players from Greytown. Then:

$$\frac{B}{B+G} \times \frac{B-1}{B+G-1} + \frac{G}{B+G} \times \frac{G-1}{B+G-1} = \frac{1}{2}$$

From which $B^2 + G^2 - 2BG - B - G = 0$, so $(B - G)^2 = B + G$.

Similarly for the second event, assuming B' players from Bluetown and G' players from Greytown, $(B' - G')^2 = B' + G'$.

We are told that $(B' + G') - (B + G) = 2 \times 24$, so it follows that $(B' - G')^2 - (B - G)^2 = 48$. The only pairs of perfect squares that differ by 48 are {1, 49}, {16, 64}, and {121, 169}. The first and third of these solutions are inadmissible because B', G,' B, and G are even numbers, so the second event had 64 players.

To check, three pairs from one town and five pairs from the other would mean 16 players and give the required probability of 50%. Similarly, 14 pairs from one town and 18 pairs from the other would mean 64 players and also give the required probability of 50%.

puzzle 36

The value of 1988 pound coins is £1,988, which is £5 more than £1,983.

puzzle 37

There are 26 former committee members (9 of whom are men), 27 committee members, and 39 members who have never been on the committee. This gives a total of 92 members.

puzzle 38

One, one, nine, three and nine.

puzzle 39

Each person consumed eight items, so Tom sold seven items to Harry, and Dick sold one. Thus Tom should receive seven coins from Harry, and Dick just one.

puzzle 40

95,759

puzzle 41

By changing his mind, B improved his chances of winning the game from ½ to ⅞.

The only way in which the first occurrence of TTT can appear before HTT is if the first three throws of the die are TTT, otherwise the sequence TTT must be preceded by an H. The probability of the first three throws being TTT is $(½)^3$, so if B chooses HTT when A has chosen TTT, then B wins with probability ⅞. If B had not changed his mind and stayed with his choice of HHH in response to A's choice of TTT, then B's chance of winning would have been ½.

puzzle 42

There are 120 seats: 85 non-aisle seats and 35 aisle seats. It is not necessary for the number of aisle seats to be an even number.

puzzle 43

White wins not by playing b4xa5, b6 or f5, which are three of the four options open to White, but by playing b5xa6 e.p.

Black's last move was a7-a5. It could not have been a6-a5 since a pawn at a6 would have had to capture White's pawn. Neither could it have been b6xa5 since this would imply, given the position of Black's other pawns, that Black had made nine captures, which is impossible since White still has eight pieces on the board. White wins as follows:

1. b5xa6 e.p.	b7xa6	
2. b5	a6xb5	and White is stalemated, which in
3. f5	any	Losers' Chess is a win for White.

puzzle 44

22 = (√.7̄ + (√7 x 7)) / √.7̄

puzzle 45

The box with the treasure is Box 3.

puzzle 46

C	D	X	C	I	V	D
L	V	M	M	I	I	L
X	C	I	X	D	X	V
I	C	C	X	C	I	I
C	M	L	X	X	I	X
X	I	I	I	V	C	I
I	X	X	X	I	I	I

puzzle 47

David, of course. Read the question!

puzzle 48

Despite being the worst shot of the three, Arthur has the best chance of surviving, with a probability of .5222. Allwyn has the next best chance of surviving at .3, and Aitkin the least chance at .1778.

Arthur's tactic will be to aim to miss if the other two are alive. This is because the other two, if they get the choice, will fire at each other rather than Arthur. This will leave Arthur with the first shot at the survivor. The reason that Allwyn would choose to fire at Aitkin rather than Arthur is that he would rather have Arthur shooting at him with a 50% hit rate than Aitkin with an 80% success rate. The decision for Aitkin to fire at Allwyn rather than Arthur, if he gets the choice, is because for Aitkin to fire successfully at Arthur would be to sign his own death warrant.

puzzle 49

The first calculation gives an unexpectedly round number.

$$3\tfrac{1}{8} \times 3\tfrac{1}{5} = \tfrac{25}{8} \times \tfrac{16}{5} = 10$$

The second calculation provides the answer:

$$3 \times \sqrt[3]{37} = \sqrt[3]{(27 \times 37)} = \sqrt[3]{999} < \sqrt[3]{1000} = 10$$

Thus $3\tfrac{1}{8} \times 3\tfrac{1}{5} > 3 \times \sqrt[3]{37}$.

puzzle 50

$$\frac{5}{34} + \frac{7}{68} + \frac{9}{12} = 1$$

puzzle 51

Name the five inventors N, O, P, Q and R, and mark their respective inventions as n, o, p, q and r, where "r" represents the robot. The table below shows the 13 crossings required.

	Starting Bank NOPQR, nopqr	Opposite Bank –
1	NOPQR, pq	nor
2	NOPQR, pqr	no
3	NOPQR, q	nopr
4	NOPQR, qr	nop
5	QR, qr	NOP, nop
6	NQR, nqr	OP, op
7	NQ, nq	OPR, opr
8	NOQ, noq	PR, pr
9	noq	NOPQR, pr
10	noqr	NOPQR, p
11	q	NOPQR, nopr
12	qr	NOPQR, nop
13	–	NOPQR, nopqr

puzzle 52

93 and 87. When the digits in each number of the sequence are reversed, the sequence is multiples of 13; that is, 13, 26, 39, 52, 65, 78 and 91.

puzzle 53

$153 = 1! + 2! + 3! + 4! + 5!$ and $153 = 1^3 + 5^3 + 3^3$.

puzzle 54

AAKAAKKK.

puzzle 55

AAKAQKJQAQKKQJJJ.

puzzle 56

Four voucher denominations are required: 1, 3, 9 and 27. Some examples:
to pay 40, use 1 + 3 + 9 + 27; to pay 25, use 27 + 1 and get change of 3; to pay 20, use 27 + 3 and get change of 9 + 1; to pay 15, use 27 and get change of 9 + 3.

puzzle 57

Suppose the first drop is from floor n. If the crystal breaks, then there is no alternative to dropping the second crystal from floor 1, floor 2, and so on, up to floor (n – 1) at most. This would ensure that no more than n drops would be required.

If the crystal does not break on its drop from floor n, then the second drop is from floor (2n – 1). If the crystal breaks here, then the second crystal is dropped from floor n + 1, up to floor (2n – 2) at most. Again this ensures no more than n drops in total.

If the crystal does not break on its drop from floor (2n – 1), continue advancing up the building as required by one less floor each time, that is, by (n - 2) floors, (n - 3) floors, and so on.

We know that a crystal dropped from the 106th floor will shatter. Thus we need to find the smallest value of n such that $n + (n – 1) + (n – 2) + ... + 1 = n(n+1)/2 \geq 105$.

The smallest value of n to satisfy $n(n + 1) \geq 210$ is 14, so the first drop should be from floor 14, and the maximum number of drops required to ascertain the lowest floor from which a crystal can be dropped so that it will shatter is also 14.

puzzle 58

Each number is put in a column according to the number of letters it has when it is written as an English word. The first column contains all the numbers with three letters, the second column has all the numbers with four letters, and so on.

"Eleven" and "twelve" have six letters when written as words, so they would appear in a fourth column.

puzzle 59

The trees are planted as follows:

There are six rows of four trees.

```
T           T

T   T   T   T

T   T   T   T

T           T
```

puzzle 60

Four and five. The numbers are the numbers of letters in the words of the question.

puzzle 61

Apart from using the information given directly, clues can be combined for extra information. For example, clues one and three can be combined to deduce that Anika is not from Woolwich. Working through, the result below then follows.

Manager	Account	District	Children
Anika	Aviation	Croydon	4
Bakkar	Marine	Woolwich	3
Charu	Liability	Brixton	5
Dhaval	Fire	Enfield	1
Ebba	Automotive	Fulham	0
Felix	Property	Lambeth	2

puzzle 62

1	0	2	0	6	6	1
3	5	0	5	5	5	6
1	3	2	2	3	1	4
1	2	5	5	3	3	1

2	2	4	0	1	4	2
4	4	4	3	0	1	1
0	0	6	0	3	5	4
2	6	0	0	3	5	2

5	1	6	6	2	2	5
3	2	2	5	3	4	0
4	2	1	1	4	4	2
5	6	2	1	5	4	5

6	0	3	1	4	4	6
3	0	5	3	0	3	1
4	5	1	6	0	6	6
6	6	3	4	3	0	6

puzzle 63

Adjacent missiles start the journey $\sqrt{50^2 + 50^2} = 70.71$ miles apart, and by symmetry move at a constant 90° angle to the next. Therefore, with a range of 70 miles the missiles will self-destruct and will not collide, and the power station will not be destroyed.

puzzle 64

		7	7	5
			3	3
	2	3	2	5
2	3	2	5	
2	5	5	7	5

puzzle 65

Take 9 coins from bag A, 12 from bag B, and 13 from bag C. No coins are taken from bag D. Weigh these coins and calculate the difference between their weight and the weight of 34 genuine coins. Each possible difference can be accounted for with exactly one pairing of bags (as shown in the table below), making it possible to identify which bags contain counterfeit coins.

In the table below, "A + 2B" indicates that the coins in bag A were overweight or underweight by one gram, and that the coins in bag B were overweight or underweight (whichever is the same as bag A) by two grams. Similarly, "A – B" means that the coins in bag A were overweight or underweight by one gram, and that the coins in bag B were underweight or overweight (whichever is the opposite of bag A) by one gram. When D is one of the counterfeit bags, all we know about it is that the coins in it are counterfeit; we don't know whether they are overweight or underweight.

Weight Difference	Explanation	Weight Difference	Explanation	Weight Difference	Explanation
1	B – C	12	B + D	26	2C + D
2	2B – 2C	13	C + D	30	2A + B
3	A – B	14	B – 2C	31	2A + C
4	A – C	15	A – 2B	33	A + 2B
5	2A – C	17	A – 2C	35	A + 2C
6	2A – B or 2A – 2B	18	2A + D	37	2B + C
6	2A – B or 2A – 2B	21	A + B	38	B + 2C
8	2A – 2C	22	A + C	42	2A + 2B
9	A + D	24	2B + D	44	2A + 2C
11	2B – C	25	B + C	50	2B + 2C

puzzle 66

Regrouping the sequence as 20, 21, 22, 23, 24, 25, 26, 27, 28, it is obvious the next three terms in this more normal format are 29, 30 and 31. Using the question's format, the required answer is 293 and 031.

puzzle 67

The answer is 204. There is one square measuring 8 x 8, 2^2 squares measuring 7 x 7, 3^2 squares measuring 6 x 6, and so on up to 8^2 squares measuring 1 x 1. This gives a total number of squares of $1 + 2^2 + 3^2 + 4^2 + 5^2 + 6^2 + 7^2 + 8^2 = 204$.

puzzle 68

The maximum number of properties owned by the property investor is 27, being 10 + 9 + 8, and the minimum number is 6, being 3 + 2 + 1. The number of possibilities for sharing from 6 to 27 properties among three people, with no two having the same number of properties, is 120.

As knowing the total number of properties and her own inheritance was insufficient for any of the daughters to deduce her sisters' inheritances, the totals of 6, 7, 26 and 27 can be eliminated immediately. That leaves 116 possibilities.

The eldest daughter is initially unable to deduce the inheritances of her two sisters. This eliminates combinations such as 8/7/5, where the eldest daughter, knowing both the amount of her own inheritance and the total number of properties, could have deduced each of her sister's inheritances. This brings us to 92 possibilities.

Continuing in this vein, after six "no" answers, we have 30 possibilities:

Total	Possible Combinations for Each Total						
15	9/5/1	9/4/2	8/6/1	8/5/2	8/4/3	7/6/2	7/5/3
16	10/5/1	10/4/2	9/6/1	9/5/2	9/4/3	8/6/2	8/5/3
17	10/6/1	10/5/2	9/7/1	9/6/2	9/5/3	8/7/2	8/6/3
18	10/6/2	10/5/3	9/7/2	9/6/3	9/5/4	8/7/3	8/6/4
19	10/6/3	9/7/3					

Because the eldest daughter was able to deduce the inheritances of her two sisters at this stage, we can deduce that the total inheritance was 19 properties. To determine whether the distribution was 10/6/3 or 9/7/3, we must look at the eldest daughter's statement that the last two answers (both "no") gave her some information, and see what she would have deduced, knowing that the total inheritance was 19 properties.

	Possibilities Remaining				
After 4 noes	10/7/2	10/6/3	9/8/2	9/7/3	9/6/4
After 5 noes	10/7/2	10/6/3	9/7/3	9/6/4	
After 6 noes	10/6/3	9/7/3			

Although the fifth "no" helps us (allowing us to eliminate the combination 9/8/2), it would only have provided information to the eldest daughter if she had been told she was inheriting nine properties. Thus the answer is nine properties for the eldest daughter, seven for the middle daughter, and three for the youngest.

puzzle 69

You don't need to know the location of Secret Place to find the treasure. Wherever you stand to follow the instructions, you will end up directly over the treasure. It is buried at a point that can also be found by walking half the distance from Crossbones Rock to Hangman's Tree, turning 90° left, and walking the same distance again.

puzzle 70

Position	Team	Captain	Uniform
1	United	Cooke	Red
2	Rovers	Allen	Blue
3	County	Dixon	White
4	Albion	Evans	Yellow
5	Thistle	Boyle	Green

puzzle 71

If the first cube had been totally submerged before the second cube was placed on the pond floor, then the second cube would also have raised the water level by three inches. The second cube raised the water level by four inches, so the first cube was not totally submerged before the second cube was placed.

If the first two cubes had been totally submerged before the third cube was placed on the pond floor, then the third cube would have raised the water level by less than four inches. This is the case because it would have taken the submersion of all of cube two and part of cube one to raise the water level four inches. Therefore the first and second cubes were not fully submerged when the third cube was placed.

If the three cubes were not fully submerged after the third cube was placed, then the water level would have risen by more than four inches. As the water level did not rise by more than four inches, all three cubes must have been submerged once the third cube was placed on the pond floor.

Let A be the area of the pond's base, s be the length of one of the cubes' sides, and x be the depth of the pond before the cubes were added. We then have:

$$3A = s^2(x + 3)$$
$$7A = s^2(x + 7) + s^2(x + 7)$$
$$11A = s^3 + s^3 + s^3$$

Multiplying the first equation by 7 and the second equation by 3, and then dividing each by s^2, we get $7x + 21 = 6x + 42$, hence $x = 21$.

Substituting for x in the first equation, $A = 8s^2$, and substituting for A in the third equation, $s = 11 \times 8 \div 3 = 29.33$ inches.

(For the sake of completeness, $A = 8s^2 = 8 \times 29.33^2$ square inches = 47.8 square feet.)

puzzle 72
The terms in the series are 10 in base 10, 20 in base 9, 30 in base 8, and so on up to 60 in base 5. The next term in the series is 70 in base 4, which is 1,012.

puzzle 73
$1! + 4! + 5! = 145$.

puzzle 74

1	1	2	2	1	3
6	3	4	4	3	6
	5	6	6	5	
	1	0	0	5	
5	2	3	3	2	5
1	1	5	5	1	4

0	4	5	4	2	4
3	0	5	1	0	3
	4	6	4	2	
	4	1	6	2	
3	0	6	2	0	1
3	1	6	4	5	3

2	0			2	4
3	5	4	0	3	5
4	5	3	1	0	6
6	2	6	1	0	3
2	0	2	4	6	1
6	0	5	0	6	2

puzzle 75
Shade a six-by-six-by-six equilateral triangle to give 21 light and 15 dark unit triangles as shown below:

If the twelve available shapes are shaded in a similar manner, ten will be found to have an equal number of light and dark unit triangles. In the remaining two cases, there are four light and two dark (or vice versa). Therefore, whichever six different shapes are chosen, the difference between the number of light and dark triangles will not exceed four. Thus it is impossible to form any six of the given shapes into a six-by-six-by-six equilateral triangle.

puzzle 76

The middle of each tree forms a right triangle with the ends of the hedge (as does any point on the curved side). The problem is thus to find an integer less than 1,760 whose square can be expressed as the sum of two nonzero squares in 13 different ways. That integer is 1,105, so the hedge is 1,105 yards long.

Measurements from the first 13 trees to the hedge are (47, 1,104); (105, 1,100); (169, 1,092); (264, 1,073); (272, 1,071); (425, 1,020); (468, 1,001); (520, 975); (561, 952); (576, 943); (663, 884); (700, 855); and (744, 817). The measurements for the other 13 trees are the same, but with the order of the measurements reversed.

puzzle 77

There were 79 coconuts to begin with. The first woman gave one of these to the monkey and hid 26 (one-third of 78), leaving 52 coconuts. The second woman gave one of these to the monkey and hid 17 (one-third of 51), leaving 34 coconuts. The third woman gave one of these to the monkey and hid 11 (one-third of 33), leaving 22 coconuts. In the morning, there was one more coconut for the monkey, making four for the monkey in total, and seven more coconuts for each woman.

Check: total = (26 + 7) + (17 + 7) + (11 + 7) + 4 = 79.

puzzle 78

Suppose n clients were picked, with 10n names in the complete mailing list. The clients picked were numbers 1, 3, 6, 10, ... with the nth and final one being number n(n + 1)/2.

Since the final one was the last name in the index, it follows that 10n = n(n + 1)/2, whence 20 = n + 1. Thus 19 clients were chosen out of a total mailing list of 190 clients.

puzzle 79

The 3-6 horizontal cannot be in the top right corner of box 1, so the 3-3 vertical is. Thus the seven doubles are all placed vertically.

4	2	1	1	6	3
0	2	0	4	6	3
	6	3	2	6	
	1	3	3	5	
0	0	3	1	5	1
6	4	2	5	6	6

4	6			0	4
5	6	2	3	5	4
4	3	3	1	0	6
4	1	0	1	5	5
2	5	0	2	3	0
3	5	5	2	6	0

4		4	3	2	4	1
6	3	5	5	2	1	
	2	4	2	2		
	3	4	6	1		
2	4	6	0	1	0	
0	1	1	5	5	0	

puzzle 80

It is a game of Monopoly.

puzzle 81

The expression e^x has the remarkable property that when its value is plotted against x, the gradient at any point on the graph is also e^x. Thus the gradient of the graph of e^x gets very steep, very quickly. (Exponentially in fact!) See sample values of e^x in column two below:

x	e^x	x^e	$e^{x(e-1)}$
.01	1.01	0.000004	0.000995
1	2.71828	1.00	2.71828
2	7.39	6.58	8.94
2.71828	15.15	15.15	15.15
5	148.41	79.43	43.18
10	22,026.47	522.74	142.09

The values of x^e (column 3) also increase quickly, the gradient at x of that graph being the differential of x^e, which is $e^{x(e-1)}$.

The graphs of e^x and x^e cross when $x = e$, where the values and the gradients of e^x and x^e are all e^e.

Because $e^x = x^e$ when $x = e$ and the gradient of e^x is increasing faster than the gradient of x^e for $x > e$, then $e^x > x^e$ for all $x > e$.

Thus we know that e^π (=23.14) is going to be greater than π^e (=22.46) as we know that π (=3.14159) > e (=2.71828).

puzzle 62

Note that White has two queens. The minimum number of moves made by White's pieces to reach the position shown in the question is queen's pawn five moves (d4, c5, b6, a7, a8(Q)), new queen two moves (a7, e3), queen's knight two moves (c3, a4), king's knight two moves (f3, h2), king's rook two moves (h3, g3), king's rook's pawn two moves (h3, g4), king's bishop's pawn one move (f3), and king one move (f2). These total seventeen moves, and therefore account for all of White's moves. Noting that Black's missing pieces were captured on c5, b6, a7 and g4, the position after White's ninth move would have been:

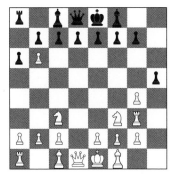

The game from White's ninth move was:

9.	...	Ra7
10.	b6xa7	h4
11.	a8(Q)	h3
12.	Qa7	h2
13.	Qe3	h1 (B)
14.	Nh2	a5
15.	Pf3	a4
16.	Kf2	a3
17.	Na4	

puzzle 63

A's hat is black. From C's statement, the sequence of the hats—with A's hat being listed first—cannot be white, white and black. This is because C, who knows that there are only two white hats in total, would then have known that his hat was black. From B's statement, A reasoned as follows: if A's hat was white, then B would have known that B's hat was black. This is because having heard what C just said, B's hat could not be white as well. Because B didn't know if B's hat was black or white, A's hat was not white and was therefore black.

puzzle 64

The formula for the area of a circle of radius r is πr^2, and the formula for the volume of a cylinder of radius r and height h is $\pi r^2 h$. Thus the answer to this question is Pi. z. z. a.

puzzle 65

The numbers in the series, as hinted in the question, can be rewritten as $1 + 1^2 + 1^3$, $2 + 2^2 + 2^3$, $3 + 3^2 + 3^3$, $4 + 4^2 + 4^3$ and $5 + 5^2 + 5^3$. The next term is therefore $6 + 6^2 + 6^3$, which equals 258.

puzzle 66

Two solutions, each using four pours, are:

	11-cup jug	13-cup jug	17-cup jug
Contents at start	9	9	9
After 1 pour	5	13	9
After 2 pours	0	13	14
After 3 pours	11	2	14
After 4 pours	8	2	17

	11-cup jug	13-cup jug	17-cup jug
Contents at start	9	9	9
After 1 pour	1	9	17
After 2 pours	0	10	17
After 3 pours	11	10	6
After 4 pours	8	13	6

puzzle 67

The terms in the series are one hundred in base ten, one hundred in base nine, one hundred in base eight, ..., one hundred in base five. The next term in the series is one hundred in base four, which is 1210.

puzzle 68

Let the train be t minutes early. The partner (driving at 36 mph) saved 5 minutes each way, so the businessman walked for $t - 5$ minutes. Because this saved 5 minutes' driving, the businessman walked at $5/(t - 5)$ of his partner's driving speed. If the partner had driven at 46 mph, the partner would have saved 4 minutes each way, so in this scenario the formula for how fast the businessman walks is $4/(t - 4)$ of his partner's driving speed. Thus:

$$\frac{5}{t - 5} \times 36 = \frac{4}{t - 4} \times 46$$

whence $t = 50$ minutes. Note: saving less time when driving 46 mph rather than 36 mph may seem counter-intuitive, but the partner would have left home later if they could average 46 mph.

puzzle 69

11, 47 and 71.

puzzle 90

6 / (1 – 5/7) = 21.

puzzle 91

We know the cats and dogs that benefitted from the will received more than $56,000 each, so in total there cannot have been more than four of them. Furthermore, we know the number of dogs and the number of cats that benefitted from the will was the same, so the total number of pets when the man died was two or four, and they received either $60,000 or $120,000 each.

Subtracting $56,000 from those amounts gives $4,000 and $64,000, but only $4,000 divides evenly into $240,000. Thus, the number of cats and dogs the man owned when he wrote his will was $240,000 ÷ $4,000 = 60.

puzzle 92

96,420 x 87,531 = 8,439,739,020.

puzzle 93

50,123 – 49,876 = 247.

puzzle 94

It is easy to overthink this puzzle. All that is required is to reposition the two matches that make the happy dog's head so that the dog is looking over its shoulder, so from < to >.

puzzle 95

Raising the numbers being compared to the power of 30, the question is whether $10^3 > 2^{10}$? The answer is "no."

puzzle 96

The integers are -3, -1 and 1.

puzzle 97

The minimum area for the smallest rectangle is (1 x 10) + (2 x 9) + (3 x 8) + (4 x 7) + (5 x 6) = 110 square units. By trial and error, the smallest rectangle meeting the requirements measures 9 units by 13 units with an area of 117 square units:

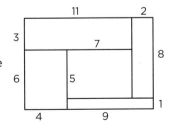

puzzle 98

The only prime factor for 1,419,857 is 17, and the first three powers of 17 that end in 7 are 17^1, 17^5 and 17^9. By inspection, $1,419,857 = 17^5$, and:

$$17^5 = (1 + 16) \times 17^4 = (1^2 + 4^2) \times 289^2 = 289^2 + 1,156^2$$

Two solutions found by using a computer for two squares that sum to 1,419,857 are: $404^2 + 1,121^2$ and $799^2 + 884^2$.

puzzle 99

Begin with the expression below:

$$1111111111 = 10$$

Between the first two digits, you may or may not place a plus sign. The same choice applies to the second and third digits, the third and fourth, and so on. As long as you place at least one plus sign, you will have a possible solution. For example, here is a way of placing plus signs that is equivalent to 2 + 3 + 1 + 4:

$$11 + 111 + 1 + 1111 = 10$$

There are $2^9 = 512$ ways of placing the plus signs, including the not-allowed option of placing none. Thus there are 512 – 1 = 511 possible equations for the kindergarten to use. As they have wall space for only 500 equations, they cannot show every possible solution using the proposed posters.

puzzle 100

Here's a lesson in water safety: the swimmer will not be able to swim back! The current doubled her speed while swimming to the boat, so when swimming against the current, she will make no progress whatsoever.

puzzle 101

1. b7xa8(N) Kxg2 2. Nb6 any 3. a8(B or Q) mate. Note that White's second move prevents 2 ... Bxa7.

puzzle 102

Suppose the army has advanced x miles before the commanding general receives the dispatch. The dispatch rider will then have ridden $x + 4$ miles.

The dispatch rider now rides $(x + 4) - 4 = x$ miles back to where the front of the army commenced its advance. The rider will arrive at this point at the same time as the rear of the army does. Thus, the rider travels $2x + 4$ miles while the army travels 4 miles.

Assuming constant speeds, the ratio of the dispatch rider's speed to the army's speed will also be constant. Thus:

$$\frac{x + 4}{x} = \frac{2x + 4}{4}$$

From which $4x + 16 = 2x^2 + 4x$ and $x = \sqrt{8}$. The dispatch rider travels $4 + 2x$ miles, so substituting for x this is 9.66 miles.

puzzle 103

$\sqrt{(6! + (6! + 6) / 6)} = 29$.

puzzle 104

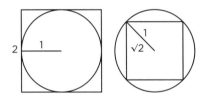

A round peg will fill a maximum of $\pi/4$ = 78.5% of a square hole. A round hole of unit radius can contain a square peg of maximum side $\sqrt{2}$, so the square peg will fill a maximum of $2/\pi$ = 63.7% of a round hole.

Thus the round peg in a square hole is the better fit.

puzzle 105

The pairs are:

355 / 113	= 3.1415929...	(π = 3.1415926...)
577 / 408	= 1.414215...	($\sqrt{2}$ = 1.414213...)
878 / 323	= 2.71826...	(e = 2.71828...)

where π is the area of a circle of unit radius and e is the base for natural logarithms.

puzzle 106

1	33/33	2	3/3 + 3/3
3	(3 + 3 + 3) / 3	4	3!/3 + 3!/3
5	3 + 3 - 3/3	6	3 + 3 + 3 - 3
7	3 + 3 + 3/3	8	3 x 3 - 3/3

9	$3 \times 3 + 3 - 3$	10	$3 \times 3 + 3/3$
11	$3! + 3! - 3/3$	12	$3 + 3 + 3 + 3$
13	$3! + 3! + 3/3$	14	$3! + 3! + 3!/3$
15	$3 \times 3 + 3 + 3$	16	$3! \times 3 - 3!/3$
17	$3! \times 3 - 3/3$	18	$3! \times 3 + 3 - 3$
19	$3! \times 3 + 3/3$	20	$3! \times 3 + 3!/3$
21	$33 - 3! - 3!$	22	$33 \times (.\dot{3} + .\dot{3})$
23	$33 - 3/.3$	24	$3 \times 3 \times 3 - 3$
25	$3^3 - 3!/3$	26	$3^3 - 3/3$
27	$3^3 + 3 - 3$	28	$3^3 + 3/3$
29	$3^3 + 3!/3$	30	$3 \times 3 \times 3 + 3$
31	$33 - 3!/3$	32	$33 - 3/3$
33	$33 + 3 - 3$	34	$33 + 3/3$
35	$33 + 3!/3$	36	$3! \times 3! + 3 - 3$
37	$3! \times 3! + 3/3$	38	$3! \times 3! + 3!/3$
39	$33 + 3 + 3$	40	$3!/.3 + 3!/.3$
41	$(3! + 3! + .3) / .3$	42	$33 + 3! + 3$
43	$33 + 3/.3$	44	$(3! + .\dot{3}) \times 3! + 3!$
45	$33 + 3! + 3!$	46	$3! \times 3! + 3/.3$
47	$3^3 + 3!/.3$	48	$3! \times 3! + 3! + 3!$
49	$\sqrt{(3!!/.3 + 3/3)}$	50	$(3! + 3 \times 3) / .3$
51	$33 + 3! \times 3$	52	$(3! + 3 - .\dot{3}) \times 3!$
53	$(3! \times 3 - .\dot{3}) \times 3$	54	$3^3 + 3^3$
55	$(3! \times 3 + .\dot{3}) \times 3$	56	$(3! + 3 + .\dot{3}) \times 3!$
57	$(3! \times 3) / .3 - 3$	58	$(3/.3 - .\dot{3}) \times 3!$
59	$(3! \times 3 - .3) / .3$	60	$33 + 3^3$
61	$(3! \times 3 + .3) / .3$	62	$(3/.3 + .\dot{3}) \times 3!$
63	$(3! \times 3) / .3 + 3$	64	$(3!/3)^{(3 + 3)}$

puzzle 107

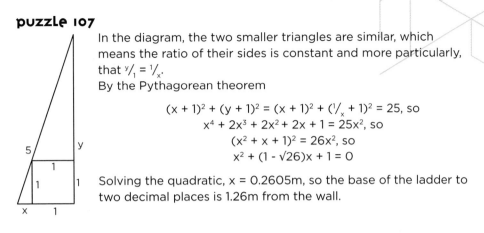

In the diagram, the two smaller triangles are similar, which means the ratio of their sides is constant and more particularly, that $\frac{y}{1} = \frac{1}{x}$.

By the Pythagorean theorem

$$(x + 1)^2 + (y + 1)^2 = (x + 1)^2 + (\tfrac{1}{x} + 1)^2 = 25, \text{ so}$$
$$x^4 + 2x^3 + 2x^2 + 2x + 1 = 25x^2, \text{ so}$$
$$(x^2 + x + 1)^2 = 26x^2, \text{ so}$$
$$x^2 + (1 - \sqrt{26})x + 1 = 0$$

Solving the quadratic, x = 0.2605m, so the base of the ladder to two decimal places is 1.26m from the wall.

puzzle 108

$12,252,239 = 2^4 \times 3^2 \times 5 \times 7 \times 11 \times 13 \times 17 - 1$

puzzle 109

The players scored 5, 7, 11, 13, 17, 19, 29, 31, 37, 41 and 43 goals. Their average was 23 goals.

puzzle 110

3	1	2	2	4	1	0	3
4	1	4	5	5	2	6	6
0	2	4			6	1	0
5	0	1			5	6	0
6	5	4	3	2	1	3	3
3	3	1			5	2	1
		3	3	6	0		
		5	2	0	6		
		5	2	4	6		
		3	0	4	4		

3-4 (and similarly 1-2) cannot be in row 5, because both ones in row 6 would then need to be 1-3. Thus 3-4 must be in column 1 and the extra double is 3-3.

puzzle 111

6	2	2	2	0	5	2
1	3	2	3	4	2	4
5	5	3	1	1	0	4
3	4	3		4	5	0
1	1	6	5	0	0	6
1	4	1	5	4	1	3
2	0	2	3	6	6	0

Row 3, column 5 must be a 1. Row 2, column 3 must be a 2. Missing dominoes: 0-5, 3-6, 4-6 and 5-6.

puzzle 112

3,816,547,290.

puzzle 113

Lemons can only be removed from the box in pairs. There is an odd number of lemons to start with, so the last piece of fruit in the box will be a lemon.

puzzle 114

The passenger on the fast train sees all the trains going the other way around that left up to three hours ago or that will leave in the next two hours. The passenger on the slow train sees all the trains going the other way around that left up to two hours ago or that will leave in the next three hours. In five hours, including the beginning and end, 21 trains depart in each direction. Including the train they are traveling on, each passenger therefore sees 22 trains on their journey.

puzzle 115

To identify the numbers we are told that we would have to know their product and the smallest number. Since knowledge of the product by itself would not allow us to determine the four numbers, the product must be obtainable in more than one way. A list of such numbers whose factors total less than 18 is given below:

Product	1st Possibility	2nd Possibility	3rd Possibility
48	1, 2, 3, 8	1, 2, 4, 6	
60	1, 2, 3, 10	1, 2, 5, 6	1, 3, 4, 5
72	1, 2, 4, 9	1, 3, 4, 6	
80	1, 2, 4, 10	1, 2, 5, 8	
84	1, 2, 6, 7	1, 3, 4, 7	
90	1, 2, 5, 9	1, 3, 5, 6	
96	1, 2, 6, 8	1, 3, 4, 8	
120	1, 3, 5, 8	1, 4, 5, 6	2, 3, 4, 5

If the smallest number were 1, then knowledge of this fact with knowledge of the product would still not be sufficient to determine the four numbers. Therefore the smallest number cannot be 1 and, by elimination, must be 2. It follows that the product is 120 and the integers are 2, 3, 4 and 5.

puzzle 116
The birthdays being celebrated were 12, 15 and 18. On the first occasion the birthdays being celebrated were 3, 6 and 9. On every birthday, the middle child has an age that is half the sum of the other two ages.

puzzle 117
The solutions are 1,872,549,630 and 7,812,549,630, and are derived as follows. The 5 and 0 can be placed immediately. The sixth digit must be 4, and as the seventh digit is odd (since every second digit must be even), it must be 9. The eighth digit must be 6. The ninth digit must be 3. The third digit is 1 or 7, so the fourth digit must be 2. The first three digits are therefore 187 or 781.

puzzle 118
Regrouping the series starting at 1, it doubles each time: 1, 2, 4, 8, 16, 32, 64, 128 and 256. In this form the next two terms in this series are 512 and 1024. To fit the pattern displayed requires a four-digit number. The answer to the question is therefore 5121.

puzzle 119
The product is 12.

From statement 1 there must be at least two ways for P to have the product he has. The possibilities are:

$$4 \ (= 1 \times 2 \times 2 \text{ or } 1 \times 1 \times 4)$$
$$8 \ (= 2 \times 2 \times 2 \text{ or } 1 \times 2 \times 4)$$
$$12 \ (= 2 \times 2 \times 3 \text{ or } 1 \times 3 \times 4)$$
$$16 \ (= 2 \times 2 \times 4 \text{ or } 1 \times 4 \times 4)$$
$$20 \ (= 2 \times 2 \times 5 \text{ or } 1 \times 4 \times 5)$$

The respective sums for these are 5, 6, 6, 7, 7, 8, 8, 9, 9 and 10.

From statement 2 the sum is not 5 (= 1 + 2 + 2) or 10 (= 1 + 4 + 5), and from statement 3 the product is not 4 or 20, so the possibilities for the product are now:

$$8 \ (= 2 \times 2 \times 2 \text{ or } 1 \times 2 \times 4)$$

$$12 \, (= 2 \times 2 \times 3 \text{ or } 1 \times 3 \times 4)$$
$$16 \, (= 2 \times 2 \times 4 \text{ or } 1 \times 4 \times 4)$$

With respective sums of 6, 7, 7, 8, 8 and 9.

From statement 4 the sum is not 6 (= 2 + 2 + 2) or 9 (= 1 + 4 + 4), and from statement 5 the product is not 8 or 16, so it must be 12.

We do not know whether this is because $2 \times 2 \times 3 = 12$ or $1 \times 3 \times 4 = 12$, but S, who knows the sum, would have known.

puzzle 120

There are five ways that Wink can win the best of nine games: 5-0, 5-1, 5-2, 5-3, or 5-4. The respective probabilities of these are: $(1/_3)^5$, $(1/_3)^5 \times 2/_3 \times 5$, $(1/_3)^5 \times (2/_3)^2 \times 15$, $(1/_3)^5 \times (2/_3)^3 \times 35$, and $(1/_3)^5 \times (2/_3)^4 \times 70$. These total 14.5%.

For Wink to win from being down 3-2, he must win three games in a row, or three out of the next four. The probability of this is $(1/_3)^3 + (1/_3)^3 \times 2/_3 \times 3 = 11.1\%$.

Wink should not accept Tiddle's offer. Tiddle could just as well have said, "In nine games, I expect to win 6–3; shall we call it 5–4?" By not accepting Tiddle's offer, Wink risks losing by 5-0 or 5-1, but also leaves more room for luck to work to his advantage.

puzzle 121

Let a, b, and c represent the sides of the triangle. We know that $a^2 + b^2 = c^2$ and $ab = 666{,}666 \times 2 = 2^2 \times 3^2 \times 7 \times 11 \times 13 \times 37$.

Either a or b is divisible by 37. Since a and b are interchangeable at this point, let us just say that a is the one divisible by 37, and that $a' = a / 37$. Since $a \geq 666$, then $a' \geq 18$. Since $b \geq 666$ and $ab = 666{,}666 \times 2$, then $a \leq 2{,}002$ and $a' \leq 54$.

As a and b (and therefore a' and b) do not share a common factor, possible factors of a' are 4, 7, 9, 11, and 13. Since $18 \leq a' \leq 54$, then $a' = 28, 36, 44,$ or 52, meaning that $a = 1{,}036, 1{,}332, 1{,}628,$ or $1{,}924$.

By elimination, $a = 1{,}924$, $b = 693$, and c (the hypotenuse) $= 2{,}045$.

puzzle 122

$545 + 5 = 550$

puzzle 123

There are 47 triangles in total, as listed below:

1 triangle of full size; 6 triangles of $1/_2$ size

3 triangles of $\frac{1}{3}$ size; 10 triangles of $\frac{1}{4}$ size
6 triangles of $\frac{1}{6}$ size; 12 triangles of $\frac{1}{8}$ size
3 triangles of $\frac{1}{12}$ size; 6 triangles of $\frac{1}{24}$ size

puzzle 124

3	4	0	4	6	2	3
5	4	3	1	1	4	4
0	2	2	6	6	3	3
2	1	5		3	6	5
5	6	6	3	1	0	1
6	5	1	4	3	2	1
1	0	5	4	2	5	5

Row 1, column 7 must be a 3. Row 4, column 7 must be a 5. Row 3, column 1 must be a 0. Missing dominoes: 0-0, 0-4, 0-6 and 2-2.

puzzle 125

Rewriting each ANNE in base ten, we have:

$$A(8^3 - 5^3 - 7^3) + N(8^2 + 8 - 5^2 - 5 - 7^2 - 7) + E(1 - 1 - 1) = 0, \text{ so}$$
$$44A - 14N - E = 0$$

Noting that A, N and E are all digits of a number written in base five, so A, N and E are all less than five, A = 1, N = 3 and E = 2 is the unique solution. Thus the three letters do represent three different digits.

puzzle 126

D scored two goals in total, but did not win a game. D scored no goals against A (no team did), at most one goal against B (who only conceded one goal in its three games), and at most one goal against C (two or more goals against C would have given D a win). D's score against C was therefore 1:1 as it could not have been 1:0.

We are told that D drew one game and lost its other two. As D drew against C it lost to B, so D's score against B was 1:2.

All of B's goals, for and against, were in its match against D, so B's games with A and C were both 0:0.

By subtraction, A's scores against both C and D were 2:0. The results are summarized below:

A vs B	A vs C	A vs D	B vs C	B vs D	C vs D
0 - 0	2 - 0	2 - 0	0 - 0	2 - 1	1 - 1

puzzle 127

Let the longer candle burn at L cm per hour and the shorter candle at S cm per hour. Then the longer candle was 8L cm, the shorter candle 8.75S cm, and 8L = 8.75S + 2.

At 8pm the candles were the same length, so 4L = 5S. Solving with the above, $S = {}^8/_5$ and L = 2, so the longer candle was 16 cm and the shorter candle was 14 cm.

puzzLe 128

	Your hand	Opponent 1	Dummy	Opponent 2
♣	10 9 8 7 5 4 2	A K Q J	-	6 3
♦	-	J 10 9 8	5 4 3 2	A K Q 7 6
♥	-	A J 3 2	10 9 8 7	K Q 6 5 4
♠	A 10 8 6 4 2	K	J 9 7 5 3	Q

Spades are trumps. If the defence leads with a diamond or a heart, ruff with a low spade and lead the ace of spades. If the defence leads a trump, win with the ace and lead a club for dummy to ruff. If the defence leads a club, ruff in dummy, then lead a trump to your ace.

Continue leading any suit other than spades and cross-ruffing. After the dummy wins the fourth club lead with a ruff, dummy will have no trumps left. You ruff dummy's lead one last time, and then whatever card you lead cannot be beaten.

puzzLe 129

Tane asks his father to take the first batch. If Taika leaves his son runners of one type, or an equal number of runners of each type, then Tane takes the remaining runners, and doubles his allowance. In any other situation, Tane can remove sufficient runners to ensure that his father has to select from one of the following combinations:

$$1, 2 \qquad 3, 5 \qquad 4, 7 \qquad 6, 10 \qquad 8, 13 \qquad 9, 15$$

This strategy is repeated as necessary for a maximum of seven times.

puzzLe 130

Ask A, "Does B tell the truth more often than C?" If the answer is yes, then ask C the next two questions, and if the answer is no, ask B. This question is designed to ensure that the second and third questions will not be directed at the goblin who lies at random.

Question two is: "Do the other two always give the same answer?" As the truthful answer is always "no," this question determines whether the goblin being asked is the one that is always truthful or the one that always lies.

Question three is: "Of the other two, does A tell the truth more often?" The answer will enable you to determine the status of the other two goblins.

puzzle 131

The numbers in the table below are the weights of the three people and the weight.

Basket 1	Basket 2
60 down	Nothing up
60 up	72 down
84 down	72 up
Nothing up	60 down
156 down	60 + 84 up
Nothing up	60 down
72 down	60 up
Nothing up	60 down
84 down	72 up
60 up	72 down
60 down	Nothing up

puzzle 132

4	6	0	0	0	1
1	5	0	2	2	6
5	0	1	1	6	3
3	6	1	5	0	0
4	4	6	3	5	3
6	2	6	4	2	6

2	0	5	6	1	3
3	2	4	2	5	2
3	6	1	2	3	3
4	1	5	5	0	5
0	2	6	1	6	4
5	3	4	3	5	4

The blanked-out dominoes were placed horizontally.

5	0	1	2	5	4
1	2	3	0	5	3
6	0	6	1	1	0
4	1	5	0	2	4
2	4	3	4	5	4
3	2	4	0	2	3

1	1		6	6
6	6	OR	1	1

puzzle 133

The answer is 111,111,111, and is guessable given this pattern: $11^2 = 121$; $111^2 = 12,321$; $1,111^2 = 1,234,321$; etc.

puzzle 134

The numbers correspond to the alphabetical positions of the letters I, V, X, L, D and M; that is, the letters that are used in Roman numerals written in ascending order of value. The missing letter is C, which in this sequence corresponds to 3.

puzzle 135

Spot could be anywhere. This is obvious if you reverse the walk.

puzzle 136

$(8 - \sqrt{9})! \times (.9 + \sqrt{.1}) = 120 \times (.9 + .\dot{3}) = 108 + 40 = 148$.

puzzle 137

The first school had 495 pupils, of which 286 were boys. The two schools combined had 1,495 pupils, of which 415 were boys.

puzzle 138

Let the dimensions of the doorway be x by y feet, then:

$$1.25 (2x + 2y) = xy, \text{ from which}$$
$$xy - 2.5x - 2.5y = 0, \text{ so}$$
$$(x - 2.5)(y - 2.5) = 6.25.$$

The only integral solutions to this equation are x = y = 5, and x = 15 and y = 3 (or vice versa). Because the doorway is higher than it is wide, the solution of x = y = 5 is rejected. The height of the doorway for the giraffe house is 15 feet.

puzzle 139

The sum of the fourth powers of the digits in the number equals the number. For example, $1^4 + 6^4 + 3^4 + 4^4 = 1,634$.

puzzle 140

Yes: one, nine, three, nine, three and nine.

puzzle 141

Our answer is **1.** d4 d5 **2.** Qd3 Qd6 **3.** Qh3 Qh6 **4.** Qxc8 mate.

puzzle 142

There is just one other such triangle, and it measures 6 x 8 x 10.

puzzle 143

7	0	3	1	5
8	2	1	9	9
4	5	8	6	4
3	2	0	7	6

puzzle 144

An infinite number of times.

puzzle 145

149, 263 and 587, which sum to 999.

puzzle 146

$73 = (\sqrt{\sqrt{\sqrt{4}}})^{4!} + (4/.\dot{4})$ and $89 = \{(4! / \sqrt{.\dot{4}}) - .4\} / .4$

puzzle 147

18, since $18^3 = 5,832$ and $18^4 = 104,976$.

puzzle 148

Whoever served first would have served on 20 of the points played, and the other player would have served on 17 of them. Suppose the first player won x of the points on which he served, and y of the points served by his opponent. The total number of points lost by the player who served them is then 20 – x + y, which must equal 13, since we are told that 24 of the 37 points were won by the player serving. Thus x = 7 + y, and the first server won (7 + y) + y = 7 + 2y points in total. This is an odd number, and only Smith won an odd number of points. Thus, Smith served first.

puzzle 149

The average speed in the first second is 12 inches per second, so assuming constant acceleration, the car's speed at the end of the first second was 24 inches per second. At the end of five seconds, the car would have accelerated to 5 x 24 = 120 inches per second for an average speed over the 5 seconds of 60 inches per second. The distance covered in 5 seconds is therefore 300 inches or 25 feet.

puzzle 150

The dominoes in Box 2 cannot all be vertically placed, or there would be two vertical 0-2s. Similarly with Box 3 (two vertical 0-0s) and Box 4 (two vertical 1-2s).

6	6	1	5	6	2	1
2	5	3	1	0	0	4
5	3	1	0	4	4	5
0	2	6	4	6	3	3

0	1	0	2	4	0	0
4	3	2	3	4	1	3
4	0	4	1	1	1	6
1	2	5	6	5	1	3

1	3	6	0	6	2	5
1	5	5	0	4	2	2
6	0	4	5	2	4	4
3	0	6	6	2	0	5

2	5	3	5	4	1	6
1	5	6	5	3	3	6
2	3	2	5	3	4	6
4	3	1	0	0	2	2

puzzle 151

A 5 x 5 checkerboard has 13 squares of one shade and 12 of the other. The five pieces, excluding the cross-shaped piece, comprise 14 white and 11 black squares. Thus the cross-shaped piece must be used.

It is then straightforward to find the following solution (piece 1 is not used):

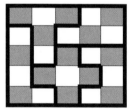

puzzle 152

The value of A is 1111, and the values of B and C are 2222 and 5555, respectively. The question is whether $B^C + C^B$ is divisible by seven. Begin as follows:

$$B^C + C^B = (B^C + C^B) + (4^C - 4^B) - (4^C - 4^B)$$
$$= (B^C + 4^C) + (C^B - 4^B) - 4^B(4^{3333} - 1)$$
$$= (B^C + 4^C) + (C^B - 4^B) - 4^B(64^{1111} - 1)$$

Since C is odd, the first term, $(B^C + 4^C)$, will be divisible by $(B + 4)$, which is divisible by seven. The second term, $(C^B - 4^B)$, is divisible by $(C - 4)$, which is also divisible by seven. Similarly, $4^B(64^{1111} - 1)$ is divisible by $(64 - 1)$, which is divisible by seven. Thus $B^C + C^B$ is divisible by seven.

puzzle 153

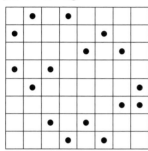

puzzle 154

10 TO 10 = 9.50

puzzle 155

Old is 30 and Young is 18.

puzzle 156

Beauden Fitzpatrick weighs 117 kg, after losing 3 kg.
Ardie Lomu weighs 113 kg, after losing 2 kg.
Dan McCaw weighs 101 kg, after losing 4 kg.
Christian Umaga weighs 111 kg, after gaining 1 kg.

puzzle 157

The murder was committed by Mrs. Peacock with a Candlestick in the Conservatory.

puzzle 158

This is a variant on the puzzle of three brothers paying £10 each for a £30 vase that has been overpriced by £5. In that version the shop assistant returns £1 to each brother and keeps £2 for himself. Thus the brothers paid £9 each, a total of £27. Add this to the £2 the shop assistant stole and that is a total of £29. Where is that missing pound? The answer is that the total spent is £25 for the vase and £2 for the shop assistant, making £27. Adding £2 to the £27 makes no sense. Ditto in the puzzle as set here. The total spent is £17 for the vase and £1 for the shop assistant, making £18, and adding £1 to the £18 makes no sense.

puzzle 159

Antipodeans may recognize that those who come from Australia have Australian pets and support Australian rugby teams, whereas Mr. White and Mr. Black, the two New Zealanders, have New Zealand pets and support New Zealand rugby teams.

NAME	HOUSE	TOWN	TEAM	PET
Mr. Gray	Blue	Wagga Wagga	Waratahs	Kangaroo
Mr. Brown	Maroon	Woy Woy	Brumbies	Koala
Mr. Green	Mauve	Bong Bong	Rebels	Kookaburra
Mr. Black	Yellow	Peka Peka	Hurricanes	Kiwi
Mr. White	Red	Aka Aka	Crusaders	Kea

puzzle 160

The order is: {2, 78, 156, 39, 4}, which can be achieved in five moves. There are three solutions using seven moves, being {4, 39, 156, 78, 2}, {3, 58, 174, 29, 6} and {6, 29, 174, 58, 3}.

puzzle 161

8	1	1	2	3	4	2
4	2	6	8	0	8	4
4	2	2	4	1	6	2
5	6	8	0	2	4	4
2	1	4	1	5	0	6
2	4	5	2	7	4	8
4	2	2	2	6	2	4